MW00698350

JUST THE GOOD STUFF

No-BS Secrets to Success . . .

(NO MATTER WHAT LIFE THROWS AT YOU)

HARMONY

NEW YORK

JUST THE
GOOD
STUFF

JIM VANDEHEI, COFOUNDER OF
AXiOS AND POLITICO

Copyright © 2024 by Jim VandeHei

All excerpts from Finish Line Copyright © 2022–2023 Axios Media, Inc.

All rights reserved.
Published in the United States by Harmony Books, an imprint of Random House, a division of Penguin Random House LLC, New York.
harmonybooks.com

HARMONY and the Circle colophon are registered trademarks of Penguin Random House LLC.

Library of Congress Cataloging-in-Publication Data is available.

ISBN 978-0-593-79637-5
Ebook ISBN 978-0-593-79639-9

Printed in the United States of America

Book design by Elina Cohen
Jacket and cover design: Anna Bauer Carr
Jacket art based on an illustration by SketchStudio/Shutterstock

10 9 8 7 6 5 4 3 2 1

First Edition

TO AUTUMN, SOPHIE, JAMES, AND KELVIN.

YOU ARE THE BEST STUFF.

CONTENTS

PART 2. WORK STUFF

PART 3. BOSS STUFF

PART 4. TOUGH STUFF

INTRODUCTION

I was among the most unremarkable, underachieving, unimpressive nineteen-year-olds you could have stumbled across in 1990.

Stoned more often than studying, I drank copious amounts of beer, smoked Camels, delivered pizza.

My workouts consisted of dragging my ass out of bed and sprinting to class—often late, usually unprepared.

There was a good reason my high school guidance counselor told my deflated parents there was no way I was college-bound: I graduated in the bottom third of my hundred-person class at Lourdes Academy in Oshkosh, Wisconsin.

I had to attend the University of Wisconsin–Menasha Extension, a two-year school, just to smuggle myself into the University of Wisconsin–Oshkosh, a four-year one in my hometown.

A year into UW-O, I was staring at a 1.491 GPA and making the guidance counselor's case daily, unambiguously, emphatically. I was one more wasted—literally and figuratively—semester away from getting the boot.

Then I yanked my head from my ass, thanks to stumbling

into two new passions: journalism and politics. (We can save for later the debate over the worst vice—politics or Jägermeister shots.)

Suddenly I had an intense interest in two new things that, for reasons I cannot fully explain, came naturally. My twin interests were animated by my innate mischievousness, contrarian impulses, long poker nights, antiestablishment bent and ease with people of all stripes at dive bars.

These passions launched me on a wild spin through media, politics, and the start-up world. It started conventionally, with small gigs at obscure publications like *New Fuels Report* and *Roll Call* turning into bigger gigs at the *Wall Street Journal* and the *Washington Post*. It thrust me through wholly unforeseeable trips through presidential impeachments and congressional coups, aboard Air Force One, onstage moderating a presidential debate, inside a wild Oval Office lunch with Donald Trump, on TV, and ultimately atop two successful media start-ups—*Politico* and Axios.

Thirty years later, I am running Axios, richer than I ever imagined, fanatical about health and self-discipline—and pretty decent at this leadership thing. My marriage is strong. My kids and family seem to like me. I still like beer. And tequila. And gin. And bourbon. But I feel, at least as of the writing of this book, I have my act together more often than not.

Thankfully for this book I took close notes as I went:

- About the type of people you ought to emulate—and the type you ought to excommunicate.

- About the values that tease out the best in people—and those that torment.

- About the hacks and habits that work—and those that people falsely *assume* work.

- About the small things it takes to thrive at your profession—and at life.

- And about the magic of having a specific plan for making the most of your gifts and opportunities, regardless of your past or present.

It is nonsense that to shine, you need to go to a fancy school, bootlick bosses, or pay your dues at crappy jobs working for bad people to rise in life. You do not need to get 1500 on your SATs or to have a sky-high IQ or family connections. You don't even need sparkling talents.

You simply need to want to construct goodness and greatness with whatever life throws at you. This starts by grounding yourself with unbreakable core values and watching, learning, and copying those who do it—and get it—right. But also by watching and studying those who screw it up.

You need to find your passions, picked by you, not imposed by others. Then outwork everyone in pursuit of shaping your destiny—your own personal greatness—on your terms, by your own measures, at your pace.

This applies to every aspect of life—your work, your health, your family, your relationships, your faith, your hobbies. They all intertwine to make you *you*. You need to map out what matters most—then throw yourself into turning wishes into reality, methodically.

You control so much more than you think. But so many often mindlessly bob along life's current. Don't.

There is an inherent hubris in writing a book of advice. You naturally come off as arrogant or a know-it-all. I am acutely aware of the shit-house luck, kind people, awesome family, and twists of fate that landed me here. And I am like so many others: an imperfect middle-of-the-pack small-town guy who worked hard, who never lost sight of life's serendipity, who feels blessed to share with others what others—or life's face slaps—shared with me. Think of me as a reporter telling the stories and secrets of people who did big or meaningful things without cutting corners, screwing over others, or being an insufferable jerk.

It is written in my favorite second language: Smart Brevity, a concept we perfected at Axios to make reading quicker, smarter, and more memorable and manageable. Hence the bullets, tight sentences, and bolded "Why it matters" callouts to give you context.

I'm a great believer in getting to the point. Throat-clearing prefaces, thunderous overtures, wordy introductions—I can't stand them. I think that puts me squarely in the majority. The times in which we live are too fast for needless noise. None of us can bear to sit through an extended drum roll before the Big Reveal.

So I've arranged this book as I've arranged my life, my head, my work, my companies—by cutting the crap and focusing on the good stuff. If I tell a story, there's a reason; if I offer an adage, there's a ton of experience or data or both behind it.

What follows is the product of decades' worth of thinking, talking, commiserating, and celebrating with friends and colleagues, then compressing and grinding all that knowledge down to just the sparkly bits. Some pieces you may recognize from my Finished Line column, but even those have been expanded and rethought. Dostoevsky and Melville and Proust were breathtaking geniuses, they produced millions of words, but they wouldn't last two hours as summer interns at Axios, where we preach the gospel of *Get to the damn point!*

That's key with daily news, but even more so with daily life. At least I think so. I am writing what I wish someone had written for me thirty years ago—a no-BS guide to the real stuff real people confront with real solutions.

My hope is you walk away with invaluable lessons—and your own plan to make the most out of life. Hopefully, you rip out pages and tack them on your wall—or pass 'em along to a friend.

The end goal: a new way of thinking about bringing the good stuff—success and richer meaning—to your own life and then to others.

HOW TO USE THIS BOOK

It took me fifty-two years to learn the lessons contained in this book. If you devour it in one sitting (as either a bowl of potato chips or a forced march), you'll miss a lot of the good stuff.

My end of the bargain: I've made each chapter super-digestible—a big idea, then examples from my life, then how-tos for you. No fluff or fat.

Your end: Since I promise not to *waste your time,* I hope you'll *take the time* to soak in the big idea and to figure out how it might serve you.

- Read a chapter, then take a walk or have a conversation. Come back later—preferably the next day.

    Maybe jot down your personal takeaways—why the big idea matters to YOU.

- This'll give you a handy reference to flip through later and see how you're doing —and remind yourself of ways to *construct your greatness.*

PART 1

I am the master of my fate:
I am the captain of my soul.

—William Ernest Henley

CHAPTER 1

ZOTHEKA!

After I'd spent fifty-one years in an artless body, my first tattoo was slapped on my right shoulder at the tail end of 2022. *Zotheka*, it reads.

WHY IT MATTERS. In Malawi, I was told, *zotheka* is considered among the most muscular words and means: "It is possible."

I had just wrapped up an unforgettable mission trip with my two sons, Kelvin and James. Local villagers would chant "Zotheka!" with infectious smiles and enthusiasm.

It nails the animating spirit of my view on work, life, health, and the purpose of this book.

You might roll your eyes at this cheesy lens.

But the mere fact that a middling dipshit like me could rise to the pinnacle of American journalism, then become CEO of two highly successful media start-ups—and then persuade you to read *this*—shows that truly *anything* is possible.

I was so middling that at my high school graduation, they had to make up an award because I had *no* scholastic, academic, or extracurricular achievements. They didn't want me to be the only kid with nothing to applaud. They called it the Campus Ministry Award because I hung out a lot in the campus ministry room, where I quickly learned I could weasel my way into random errands and sneak smokes.

Oh, and when I graduated college in a speedy 5.5 years and loaded up my VW Rabbit to hit the big time in Washington, D.C., I confidently fired off a hundred résumés before landing a job—carrying bricks for a bricklayer.

I was remarkably unremarkable.

Whether you are in high school, your early career, or your late career, or living happily retired in Florida, you should embrace the Zotheka mentality for four big reasons:

- ☛ **IT'S TRUE.** You can dog America all you want. But every person, even in the crappiest of circumstances, has the potential to do great things. Too often, people use circumstance as a crutch.

- ☛ **IT'S LIBERATING.** Once you break free of believing you are limited by education, family, location, your current job, or circumstance, you start to push yourself, take risks, reveal new dimensions.

- ☛ **IT'S INTOXICATING.** One of the tricks to life is stacking small wins on top of each other—run half a mile, then a mile, before trying to nail a half-marathon. Next thing you know, you are doing things you once thought impossible. It's addictive.

☞ **IT BEATS THE HELL OUT OF THE ALTERNATIVE.** Life is hard enough without slapping restrictions on what is possible. It's a drag to feel like a prisoner to the status quo. Oh, and no one wants to hang with a hangdog.

CHAPTER 2

CONSTRUCTING GREATNESS

Sally Jenkins, sports columnist for the *Washington Post,* captured brilliantly the secret to success in business and life:

Tom Brady, the greatest NFL quarterback ever, she wrote, "proved that any kid with perfectly ordinary athletic prospects, the middle-of-the-packer who doesn't come with some preloaded or far-fetched anatomical gift, can construct greatness. What made him great was an inner curiosity, an urge to fill in his blanks and see what might happen with enough study and sweat."

Brady was a sixth-round draft pick and considered unremarkable by most conventional measures. He willed himself into being the greatest QB ever.

WHY IT MATTERS. Okay, no shot you will be Brady. But you don't need to be born a genius or sports sensation, attend Harvard, or have friends in high places to be the very best at what you do.

You simply need to decide what matters most to you—and do the hard, daily work to make it happen.

You control *you*. So much time and angst gets wasted fixating on the past. So don't.

Graduating in the bottom third of my high school class actually motivated me and helped me appreciate a few lessons on how any of us middle-of-the-packers can beat the dealer:

☛ **THE PAST AND PEDIGREES ARE OVERRATED.** The second you hit the real world and workplace, no one gives a hoot about your college, GPA, or past mistakes or triumphs. It's all forward motion: What are you doing *now*? What can you do *next*?

☛ **DO SOMETHING YOU WOULD DO FOR FREE.** You can't fake passion. And passion leads to a healthy daily obsession. If you find a way to get paid to do what you love most, passion comes naturally. All of us should be in perpetual pursuit of a job we love doing, until kids or true obligations to others prevents it.

☛ **STEAL FROM THOSE SMARTER THAN YOU.** Be a student of those crushing what you want to crush. And copy their best habits or moves. Read. Listen to podcasts. Pick up the phone. A little trick: Call or email people you admire. You will be shocked at how generous most people are about sharing their tricks and wisdom. All of us want to be asked how we do something well. Exploit this.

☛ **SURROUND YOURSELF WITH GOODNESS AND GREATNESS.** Success is wasted if you do not find good people to both share it with and learn from. Glue yourself to people who make you better and make you feel better. Stop justifying bad bosses, friends, or partners. Glue yourself to people you admire and soak up their smarts.

☛ **GRIT IS IT**. My wife, Autumn, and I spend more time talking with our kids about this than grades or awards. There is no substitute for getting up every day and pouring uncommon time and effort into what matters most. This means sucking it up when you flop or fail. I have no tolerance for people who whine but don't grind. Don't be that person.

CHAPTER 3

YOUR STORY

Your life is a story—a long, winding, wildly unpredictable narrative. So write it. Literally.

WHY IT MATTERS. It may sound self-indulgent and grim. But you should spend more time thinking about the story of your life—the obit one day to be written. Knowing *who* we want to be and *how* we want to be seen and remembered creates a natural framework for how to live today.

I was mid-career before I learned the invaluable lesson of writing down who and what I wanted to be and taking detailed notes on people, phrases, or moments that could and should shape me.

My compilation of words, sayings, goals, eye-popping encounters, and unforgettable stories stretches thousands of pages across Word documents and files in my iPhone Notes application.

Here's a little secret. Anyone who claims nonchalance about a successful job or marriage or athletic triumph is full of it. They put tremendous forethought into making it happen.

It is not self-indulgent to craft your own narrative. Otherwise, months and years race by rudderless.

Write down:

- ☞ **WHO DO YOU WANT TO BE?** I want to be a loyal, loving, and loved husband, father, sibling, son, and friend. But I also want to seen as a smart, successful, moral dude. Oh, and I want to be fit, fly-fish, and better than the crappy golfer I am today. List yours.

- ☞ **YOUR BIG MOMENTS.** Life will smack you upside the head with illness or heartbreaks. So cherish—and document—the memories you don't want to fade. Over time, you will draw so many patterns and so much wisdom from these moments when they are stitched together.

- ☞ **WHAT YOU WISH YOU KNEW.** Since I blew off most of school, I started jotting down fancy words that befuddled me—*lachrymose, verisimilitude,* etc. It helped me fake that I wasn't a dope in D.C., then grow my vocabulary with words that you should slap me if I ever use. Later, this extended to memorable sayings or complex concepts. The mere act of writing things down helps sharpen your thinking.

- ☞ **THANK-YOU NOTES.** Take time to take note of people helping you. Be specific about what they did and how it made a difference. Keep one copy yourself. Send one to them. It will make their day.

CHAPTER 4

SHIT-HOUSE LUCK

Almost every great thing in life starts with serendipity, usually someone—or something—new entering your life by chance.

WHY IT MATTERS. This reality should humble all of us. We often celebrate big names who invent companies or pull off remarkable feats.

But the truth is that most good fortune—or big breaks—flow from dumb luck and happenstance.

This does not contradict my belief that we control far more than we think. The stuff you control merely positions you to exploit dumb luck.

My life-altering moment hit in 1993, when I pulled a full list of Wisconsin newspapers in hopes of finding an internship— anywhere, at any pay. I was twenty-two and trying to control my . . . employment.

Zane Zander, publisher of the weekly newspaper *The Brillion News*, happened to be one of my first calls on the alphabetical list of papers.

He asked me to pop up to Brillion, a small town not far from Green Bay, ASAP for a quick chat. After I explained I was new to journalism, coming off my *first* writing class, he asked me to run his entire newspaper for the summer, alone, with one week of training.

I reiterated he would be hiring a mediocre student with scant experience. But he was in a jam: His editor needed the summer off. Mr. Zander needed an immediate sub.

He offered me a pay package no cheesehead could resist: $300 per week, a car, his cottage on a pond loaded with bass, and a fridge loaded with cold beer.

There's little chance I would be writing this today absent the master's class in running a weekly newspaper Mr. Zander put me through.

My confidence and ambition soared. I took more chances, including applying for an internship in Washington, D.C., in the office of Senator Herb Kohl.

I later learned I had the lowest GPA of the applicants—but won the spot by telling my interviewers I would use the months in Washington to study inside out what I wanted to cover as a journalist when I graduated: congressional power. This was a life changer, and the experience would soon lure me to D.C., where I live to this day.

All of us have stories of simply being in the right place for luck to strike. We should cherish them. And use them to keep our egos in check.

Here's how to position ourselves for—and exploit—luck and happenstance:

- ☞ **THE MORE, THE MERRIER.** It's not totally true we make our own luck, but we sure as hell can help. The more you take chances, talk to others, throw yourself into opportunities, the better the odds of catching an unexpected break.

☛ **POUNCE ON LUCK.** When something seems like fate, it just might be. So seize the moment and squeeze as much wisdom and joy as you can from your fortuitous turns. Write down your dreams and goals, but then be flexible enough to toss away the detailed plans and roll with the wild twists when they come your way.

☛ **LUCK BEGETS LUCK.** There's often a natural momentum to life. If you surf one wave of luck, it often seems another comes crashing along to ride.

☛ **BE GRATEFUL.** Give thanks for those who help you—and look for every chance to do the same for others.

Thanks, Zane.

CHAPTER 5

THE POWER OF INSECURITY

Confession: Well, yes, that *is* a massive chip on my shoulder.

It was planted by that high school guidance counselor who told me I wasn't smart enough for college. It was fertilized by that stellar 1.491 GPA in Year 3 of college.

It sprouted fully the moment I landed in Washington, D.C., in 1995, surrounded by people with fancy pedigrees and Ivy League degrees. This was intimidating as hell for a small-town cheesehead with one Supper Club plaid sport coat and little hope for a job.

I've spent every year since, consciously or subconsciously, trying to prove I am smart enough to not just belong—but thrive.

WHY IT MATTERS. None of us wants to be insecure. But never underestimate the power your insecurity can generate if you are aware of it and exploit it healthily.

💣 **TRUTH BOMB.** Very few sane people are as confident as they seem. We are all messed up and tortured. So stop measuring your worth or confidence against others.

My insecurity inspired me to try to outwork—and outthink—those I assumed had a head start or some educational or connections edge. Truth is, most had significant edges.

Growing up in Oshkosh, I was okay, if uninspired. Okay at school. Okay at sports. Okay at work. My saving grace was two terrific parents, two terrific siblings, four grandparents, all living in my hometown. So lots of love and safety.

I truly didn't hit a groove outside of family, fun, and friends until my twenties. So by the time I rolled out of Wisconsin and into D.C., no wonder I was intimidated and unsure if I could cut it.

Truth is, we all suffer some feelings of the impostor syndrome (except the true narcissists).

Here are a few ways to attack your own impostor worries:

- ☛ **BE HONEST WITH YOURSELF.** Insecurities are often rooted in some truth. Try to understand your weaknesses, real or perceived, so you can do something about them.

- ☛ **ATTACK THOSE WEAKNESSES.** Do the small daily things to overcome the nagging insecurities. First, try to mitigate any weakness, then turn it into a strength. You will be shocked how persistence and effort can ease or erase limitations.

- ☛ **WEAPONIZE THE FURY.** Chicago Bulls star Michael Jordan famously looked for any slight by another player to manufacture motivation, knowing it provides a tiny extra edge or jolt. He was maniacal about it—but the trick does work.

Fear is a fabulous fuel. Use it.

☛ **GIVE YOURSELF GRACE.** I can't sing. I can't dance. I kinda suck at Trivial Pursuit. At some point, it's wasted energy to lament. Double down on things you do well instead.

THE BOTTOM LINE. We all carry baggage. The successful people in my life simply accept that—and do something about it. So do it. I could easily get paralyzed by my middle-of-the-pack IQ or countless Twitter critics or several very Google-able negative stories about my missteps. Or I can brush it off—and try not to screw up the next time.

CHAPTER 6

JETTISON THE JERKS

If I could change one thing about my ten years running *Politico,* it's this: wasting months of my life bitching about the bad actions of the owners and some powerful leaders who came through our doors.

We would often decamp to the office of our managing editor, Danielle Jones, who was our resident muse and shrink (think Wendy Rhoades from the television show *Billions*). We'd commiserate, complain, and eventually plot our mass exodus. Therapeutic? Yes. But what a terrific waste of time.

WHY IT MATTERS. Every hour spent exacting revenge—or bemoaning bad values—is time not spent doing and building good things with good people.

Bitterness blows. Truth is, bad people do bad things—and nothing we can do will change them.

But we can leave 'em. Or ignore 'em.

You win by doing the right things for the right reason—and ignoring the jerks, haters, and narcissists.

It's easy to get sucked into their negative energy. Here are a few hacks to avoid that:

- ☛ **JUST SAY NO.** Too many people are too timid to bluntly tell others when they are jerks or unacceptably negative. Draw—and state—boundaries. And when someone keeps crossing them . . .

- ☛ **CRUSH THE CANCER.** We choose our friends, colleagues, and main interactions. Eliminate—or at least dramatically curtail—time with anyone who sucks life out of you.

- ☛ **BE RUTHLESSLY PRAGMATIC.** People very rarely change in dramatic ways. If someone is an ass over and over, stop wishing or thinking they'll change. Chances are, an ass they shall forever be.

- ☛ **SEEK AND SAVOR THE GOOD ONES.** Most people are good. So marinate in positive relationships, at home and at work. Feed off that energy.

THE BOTTOM LINE. One of the smartest things we did when we started Axios was to make a common vow to purge anyone with bad values and motives, regardless of talent.

It has made for a happier workplace—and life. I only wish I'd learned this lesson decades earlier.

CHAPTER 7

FIND AN AUTUMN

I will never forget telling Don Graham, the mild-mannered publisher of the *Washington Post,* about our plans to start *Politico* in the summer of 2006.

"I have never said this to anyone," he fulminated in his slow, staccato style. "You are making a ca-ta-stro-phic mistake." Don's appraisal was a popular one. After all, I was chucking one of the best gigs in American journalism to try to take on the *Post* from scratch.

Thankfully, I was naive or courageous—or just plain lucky enough—to not give a shit.

Still, we almost chickened out. Don sent Bob Woodward, Ben Bradlee, and other *Post* stars to lobby John Harris, my editor and partner in crime, and me to stay. Don even offered to fund a company inside the *Post*, called Post Politics, and let us run it.

My wife, Autumn—home with two small kids—saw us buckling and fired off a note quoting Churchill and Roosevelt and told us to suck it up and grow a pair. We did.

WHY IT MATTERS. Autumn knew me well enough to know I needed a swift kick to do the risky but right thing.

We all need an Autumn—a family member, friend, or mentor whom we trust to give us wise, and often tough, advice.

She knew the risks. We had two young kids, and I was giving up a $140,000 salary for a start-up most thought would fail.

I hadn't managed anything in my life, other than the night shift at Little Caesars in my late teens. But she often knows me better than I do. She made me start *Politico*—and even came up with the name.

A few tricks for finding—and making the most of your relationship with—your Autumn:

- ☞ **ABSOLUTE TRUST.** Your coach needs to be someone you trust unequivocally. You trust their motivation, their morals, their instincts, and their track record.

- ☞ **GET VULNERABLE.** This works only if the person knows your worst flaws and deepest doubts. Most of your bad instincts and patterns flow from insecurity and fear, so stop trying to hide them. To anyone who really knows you, they are plain to see.

- ☞ **LISTEN.** It is so easy to talk yourself out of taking risks or to talk yourself into justifying the wrong thing for the wrong reason. We all need a gut check.

- ☞ **HARD TRUTHS ARE, WELL, TRUE.** Early in *Politico*, my instinct, born of my own insecurities, was to punch back hard against every critic.

    Mike Allen, who cofounded *Politico* and Axios with

me, once pulled me aside, cautioning: "We'll be in this town a long time. Make sure when you look back a few years from now, you'll be glad you did what you think you want to do."

It was his polite way of saying: Put a sock in it, hothead.

THE BOTTOM LINE. We all need coaches in our lives. Find them, hold on to them, and be more explicit in asking them for unvarnished feedback about being a better friend, teammate, sibling, child, or colleague. Then take the advice.

CHAPTER 8

DON'T BE A LOSER

I was in a fighting mood when we launched *Politico* in the winter of 2007. It felt like everyone was rooting against us, and the *Washington Post* was scrambling to undermine our debut by stealing a few of our ideas. The *Post* even floated a new site called Post Politics—an idea we had pitched in our final months as an alternative to leaving.

In public and private, we wanted a little revenge. We secretly bought the PostPolitics.com website after learning of their copycat plans. And in media interviews, I taunted them, claiming our tiny new site would be "better than the *Washington Post.*" It FELT good. But it was a loser's move.

WHY IT MATTERS. Nothing screams weakness like arguing mainly why someone or something else sucks. It often projects the opposite of what you think and hope. If you trash—or focus obsessively on—a friend, a competitor, a colleague, or a company to win . . . you're by definition losing.

Conversely, nothing shouts strength like showing why you or your ideas are better.

Always operate from a position of strength.

It took me years to fully grasp this. I often made the mistake of not just spotting the shortcomings of others but harping on them. In retrospect, that's weak.

When we launched *Politico,* the thirty-six-year-old me would too often criticize our rivals instead of simply playing up our unique strengths.

Or earlier in my career, I would sometimes fixate on why someone else sucked, rather than let my strengths speak for themselves. At *Roll Call,* where my career started to really take off, Ed Henry, then the editor and later a fallen Fox News star, was the target of my hazing. I felt certain I had better ideas for running the publication, and let his boss and others know it.

It would have been wiser to project self-confidence based on our cool idea for a new publication—or my own moves as a rising professional.

This doesn't mean you can't clinically offer assessments of competitors or people. Just don't make it your core focus and obsession.

This choice unfolds daily in business deals, internal disputes, and relationships. Here are things to watch to sniff out winners—and losers.

- ☛ **WHINERS.** People who gripe and moan about others' unfair advantages or flaws are usually exposing their own insecurities. Big red flag.

- ☛ **WHISPERERS.** You never want to do business or hang around with people who gossip about others. One day they'll gossip about you.

☛ **WEASELS.** The only thing worse than people who are so insecure that they unwittingly act with malice are those who do so with forethought. They are rodents.

☛ **WANNABES.** Watch for signs of someone talking down to someone else out of clear envy. This is a telltale sign of lack of confidence and conviction. Wannabe-ism is the gateway drug to weasel-ism.

☛ **WUNDERKINDS.** Also watch for those who brag on their own credentials or brainpower. If someone says they're smarter or better than someone else, deep down they fear they're not.

THE BOTTOM LINE. When you're selling yourself, an idea, or a product, you win by making your case on your terms—not trashing others.

CHAPTER 9

TAMING DEMONS

We all wrestle demons. Mine is a fight-or-fight impulse. No, that's not a typo—the flight thing isn't in my wheelhouse.

In conflict, I want to argue, prove myself right or righteous—and win, decisively.

You can imagine how this demon, untamed, stirs all kinds of potential trouble with my wife or with people in business.

WHY IT MATTERS. The thin, fragile line between success and failure in marriage/relationships and work is knowing and then taming your personal demons.

I'm doubtful we ever truly conquer our personal demons fully. We hide 'em. We cage 'em. But the moment we think we beat 'em, they return.

I was reminded of this after the 2023 White House Correspondents' Association annual dinner.

Michael Schaffer, a *Politico* columnist, called saying he wanted an interview about my weekly Finish Line column. My initial response: *Hell no.*

I said there was no way *Politico* would ever allow him to write positively or fairly about Axios . . . or me . . . or Finish

Line. I cofounded and ran *Politico* but left after a dispute over business values with the previous owner. We've been rivals ever since. Weird, I know.

Schaffer promised he was on the level and insisted he admired the culture inside Axios—a big focus of this column. So I bit. Our hourlong interview was thoughtful and very friendly. I kinda liked the guy. Sucker!

His *Politico* column titled, "Jim VandeHei's Surreal Wellness Evolution," was snarky and cynical. It felt like a sucker punch.

Just after it published, I found myself at a late-night party at the Swiss ambassador's residence in Washington, D.C., tequila and soda in hand. Matt Kaminski, the editor in chief of *Politico,* stood nearby.

Fight-or-fight kicked in. I put down my drink, put my hand on his shoulder, and told him the column was a "piece of shit" and that he should be ashamed for greenlighting it.

We had a spirited chat. I'm pretty sure I ended it by saying: "You are dead to me." Hat tip: Casamigos Blanco.

The result was I blew hours of my life stewing about something meaningless—then interrupted a fun night griping about it.

Was Kaminski really going to admit he or his boss ordered up a petty little cheap shot? Fat chance.

It did spark the idea to write this. And it gave me time to reflect on how any of us tame impulses:

☞ **SPOT THEM.** You can't control what you don't see. I
   knew early on the same impulse that got me kicked out

of high school science class (I was certain the teacher was a fraud) or led to disorderly conduct in college (I was certain the drinking age was too high) would get me in trouble if unchecked. You can't fix something until you admit it's broken.

☛ **UNDERSTAND THE ROOT.** We need to reckon with what fuels our worst impulses. In this case, it's probably a mix of ego, pride (I throw all of myself into things I care about, so any attack can feel like a shot at my core being), and self-righteousness.

☛ **QUIT RATIONALIZING.** It's easy to convince yourself you're simply being principled and fighting for what's right. But when that same impulse is behind most of your bad decisions, try a different lens. If a habit or tendency leads to a bad result more than once, it's gut-check time.

☛ **LISTEN TO OTHERS.** My wife, Autumn, and cofounders, Roy and Mike, are quite proficient at telling me to chill out and focus on what actually matters. We all need hard-truth tellers to hold us accountable.

☛ **REALIZE YOUR RECIDIVISM.** I am a calmer, more controlled guy at age fifty-two. I'm more disciplined and harder to stir up. But I'm still me—and my blink emotional response is to defend and debate. I kinda like confrontation. Just knowing that helps keep it in check. Sometimes.

☞ **LAUGH AT YOURSELF.** We all need to take ourselves less seriously. We can chuckle at our glitches—as long as we're aware of them and working on them. Sometimes you can even write chapters about them.

CHAPTER 10

GRATITUDE ATTITUDE

Political reporter Jonathan Swan, in his farewell Q and A with our Axios staff, said the best piece of advice he ever read was that you get back everything—and more—than you give away.

Swan, a rare media star whose generosity grew in proportion to his stardom, was talking about sharing sources, bylines, and tricks of the trade.

WHY IT MATTERS. The older I get, the more certain I am this applies to every aspect of life, particularly work. The more you give and serve others, the more *you* benefit and get ahead.

This cuts against the popular narratives of the "great man"— the daring but often uncaring entrepreneur or billionaire glass-breaker.

There's often an assumption you need a cutthroat edge or an I-don't-give-a-shit abandon to do big things fast.

⚡**REALITY CHECK.** I am *not* suggesting great success flows from being soft or merely generous. But everyone should aspire to be both great *and* generous—the twin win.

Some ways to put this into practice:

☛ **PAY IT FORWARD.** Look for *daily* opportunities to share your wisdom, secrets, and life hacks. It's ludicrous to assume doing this disadvantages you. On the contrary, it makes people cheer for you. It's a big reason I'm writing this.

☛ **GET OVER YOURSELF.** There is a 99.9999 percent chance you are not Thomas Edison or Mother Teresa. Stop thinking you are better than other people because your specific skill puts you in a position of success. Flip the script: Be grateful for your breaks and show it. Enjoy success and share it with others with reckless abandon.

☛ **SMALL THINGS MATTER.** Few people inspire others with heroic words or deeds. But small things to you are big things to others: A coffee with a new colleague. A note of encouragement. In-the-moment advice. A gentle correction or instruction. A simple thank-you.

☛ **BE INTENTIONAL.** Thank, respect, and serve people in your organization who are newer than you. We naturally suck up. But today's intern could be tomorrow's boss.

☛ **PASS IT ON.** Talk to others about how gratitude helps them get ahead. If you see an opportunity to gently rein in an ego gone wild, take it.

CHAPTER 11

BE A QUITTER

In 2009, I was recruited for one of the most prestigious and cool appointments in American journalism: to serve a customary nine-year term on the Pulitzer Prize Board at Columbia University in New York.

Three years later, I quit.

I simply couldn't dig deep into fifteen books, scores of newspaper stories, and esoteric poetry collections like *Inseminating the Elephant* every year—while trying to run a start-up, *Politico*. It was a painful call. I'm so glad I made it.

WHY IT MATTERS. The hardest—and often best and most important—decisions are what we *stop* doing. We all need to be better quitters.

We often keep doing stuff because we think we have to or we worry about what others will think.

Hell, I was part of the world's smartest book club, talking shop with living legends of my industry. And I was helping steer the most coveted awards in literature and journalism. And I knew it would seem weird to bounce early.

But once I thought about what was best for me, the answer

was obvious. Two things were far more important: my family and my day job.

So how do we know when to quit? Here's my take on this as I look back over decades of my best quits. If the position is . . .

- ☞ **LIFE-SUCKING.** If a person or job or habit is routinely sucking the life out of you, bolt. Routinely is critical. Lots of things suck episodically. But things that suck consistently gotta go. If your boss or job sucks consistently, run! There are lots of better ones out there.

- ☞ **ENERGY-DRAINING.** These situations provide real happiness—but it's outweighed by constant negativity. I realized in my final years at *Politico*, which I ran before starting Axios, that I was spending 70% of my time trying to fix or hide the bad or baffling behaviors of others. I loved so many parts of the gig. But this was the tell that it was time to go.

   💡 **HERE'S THE FORMULA.** Does a situation stir more negative energy than positive energy on a regular basis?

- ☞ **TIME-SUCKING.** We all get pulled into "must-dos" and "obligations." Some really are. Many aren't. This is where it helps to keep a literal inventory of what matters most to you. If something is eating up more time than it seems to warrant, reevaluate. This is why at Axios, we are always asking our staff to take stock of what they do and why, and we try to shrink their focus. The Pulitzers, for a slow reader like me, were a full-time job on top of a start-up life. It was too much.

☞ **BRAIN-NUMBING.** Boredom blows. It's like sleeping while awake. If you find yourself in a job or role or habit that's simply dull, move on. Yes, all this is easier said than done. But I'm struck by how many people mindlessly stick with dull stuff "just cuz."

☞ **BRAIN- OR BODY-HARMING.** We do a lot of dumb things out of habit or laziness. We eat and drink crap that drains us. We watch or engage with stuff that maddens or saddens us. We hang with people who worsen or warp us. Deep down, we know the answer: Stop doing it. So stop.

☞ **LIFE-ENHANCING.** There are positive reasons to throw in the towel, too. I had my dream job in 2006: national political reporter for the *Washington Post*. I loved it. Never thought I'd leave. But then we had the idea for *Politico*, a rare chance to create and run something. If life tosses you the chance to learn, grow, or experiment in exciting ways, pounce—and quit.

PART 2

CHAPTER 12

MAKE AND TAKE YOUR BREAK

My big Washington break came in 1996, when Susan Glasser, the editor of *Roll Call,* a small but influential newspaper covering Congress, hired me to cover congressional leadership.

Glasser's reporters were routinely stealing and rewriting stories I was breaking for a small obscure publication called *Inside the New Congress.* So I shot her a snarky note telling her if she liked my stories so much, she should hire the original. To her credit, she did. (*Lesson:* Sometimes it pays to be a smart-ass.)

WHY IT MATTERS. Glasser hired me at the very moment Congress was *the* story in Washington, with then speaker Newt Gingrich often upstaging or overshadowing sex-scandal-stained president Bill Clinton. By pure luck of timing, I had a beat the journalism world was watching closely—an authentic big break.

I had three advantages at the time: I was roughly the same age as most of the congressional aides who sat in the most important meetings. I liked to drink and play cards. And I was not an Ivy League liberal. This was a winning trifecta in a Congress controlled by Republican men.

I was also a contrarian who was obsessed with how people got, used, and abused power. And damn, did I have a front-row seat to the use and abuse of power.

While other reporters wrote the same boring stories, talking to the same boring people, I dove straight into the action—the inner sanctums of Gingrich and majority whip Tom DeLay, then the most powerful and feared man in Congress.

It paid off big-time.

I was the first reporter to discover Republican leaders were holding secret meetings in the basement of the U.S. Capitol to plot the early stages of the impeachment of Bill Clinton.

It was earthshaking news that landed me on NBC's *Today* show with Katie Couric and Matt Lauer. I was twenty-seven, looked like I was twenty-two—and wore my one sport jacket, better suited for a bowling alley than a TV set. It was not my finest moment.

Not long after, I broke the news that soon-to-be speaker of the house Bob Livingston would shock the world and resign because he was having an affair.

I had cultivated sources others did not have and asked questions others ignored. This formula would serve me well at every critical juncture, including making the shift from journalist to entrepreneur.

It sounds crazy now. But in 2006, I was thirty-five and had one of the best jobs in journalism—political reporter at the *Washington Post*—and I had a nagging feeling about political news: It felt slow, voiceless, and unmoored from the raging cable and internet era. I was certain there was a different, better, faster, smarter way.

Google bought YouTube for gobs of money that summer. It struck me: What would it cost someone with Google-like money to take on my own paper, the legendary *Washington Post*? Not much, I surmised. If someone could hire away the six or so reporters who routinely broke news and exploited the insatiable appetite of cable and internet junkies for politics, it could be done fast and cheap.

The idea—based on that one question—created *Politico,* which became arguably the most successful new media company of the internet era.

So how do you make and take your breaks?

☛ **THINK**. You need to know the general direction you're heading. Take the time to reflect on your interests and passions. What excites you? What bores you? Where are you willing to move? What is the maximum amount of risk you can stomach?

☛ **TRAIN**. You make and control your destiny more than you think. But often only if you put the hours in. This means studying the topics that interest you, meeting people and asking smart questions, and working to sharpen your strengths and dull weaknesses.

☛ **ASK**. Find mentors in every job, whether it's your dream job or one at Burger King or a stint in the mailroom. Don't be a stalker. But be curious about how things work, what worked well for them, what didn't, and what more you can learn in your current gig.

☛ **WORK.** The single best way to catch a break is to put yourself in as many situations as possible for one to materialize. This means being the person who raises their hand for any new task, no matter how menial. And it often means being the first person in, the last to leave. People want to reward effort.

☛ **POUNCE.** This is the magic. You need to have the smarts and courage to take the breaks you make. This does not mean saying yes to every opportunity. It does mean jumping at chances that fit your desired trajectory. Two great questions to ask: Will this teach me things I need to learn? Will it expose me to people I would benefit greatly from learning from? If you can answer yes to both, it's probably worth it.

CHAPTER 13

PERPETUAL PURSUIT OF HAPPINESS

My one piece of advice to anyone thinking about their future:

Persistently pursue work so personally satisfying that you would do it for free.

WHY IT MATTERS. We spend more than half our adult life at work, getting to work, thinking about work, or whining about work.

So hunt for professional happiness. Of course there may be times in your life that you need to get a paycheck simply to survive or provide for others. But never stop seeking deep meaningful work.

Noodle on this depressing data from Gallup global polling:

Gallup found that only 20 percent of us say we're thriving at work.

Some 62 percent are indifferent to their work lives; 18 percent are downright miserable.

No wonder Gallup's worldwide survey of happiness found people are sadder than ever.

Millions of Americans, including many people I know, have

little choice about their work for a variety of reasons. But millions of young college graduates and knowledge workers have more choices than at any time in the history of the planet.

My unhappiest moments came when I failed to follow my own advice. In 2013, for instance, *Politico* was a massive business success, but it was sucking the life out of me. I found myself spending 70 percent of my time in boring unnecessary meetings or in tension with Robert Allbritton, who owned the company, and John Harris, my cofounder.

Autumn was so tired of my whining, she offered one word of advice: Quit. (It took nearly three years for me to fully act on it.)

The puzzle is that so many don't act when they're unhappy— and get stuck in a totally unnecessary rut of their own making.

Here are a few things I tell my kids:

- ☛ **STUDY YOURSELF.** Yes, do your homework and get good grades. But study more closely what electrifies your mind and lights up your heart. These two signals tell you what you love.

- ☛ **DON'T LISTEN TO YOUR PARENTS.** So many kids simply do what Mom or Dad did, or what Mom or Dad wants them to do. Parents can guide and love—but they can't impose passion or joy.

- ☛ **MEANING, NOT MONEY.** A clear, well-worn path to indifference or misery is seeking a profession simply because it pays well. A lower-income teacher who loves her job will live a far better life than a rich financier who hates hers.

☞ **QUIT UNTIL YOU HIT.** This one will elicit groans. But setting artificial obligations to stay in soul-sucking jobs or majors is silly. You will have bad days. Suck it up. But if you have bad *months,* mix it up.

☞ **FIGHT BACK.** You should never settle unless you have no choice. We get one lap around life. So perpetually pursue jobs, bosses, colleagues, and work that bring maximum growth, fulfillment, and happiness.

THE BOTTOM LINE. Happy work alone does not a happy life make. But it sure as hell helps when other parts of your life are sagging or sucking.

CHAPTER 14

EXCELLENCE OVER SUCCESS

Brad McCarty—head coach of the men's soccer team at Messiah University in Mechanicsburg, Pennsylvania—is one of the winningest and dogmatically philosophical coaches in soccer.

One of the things this Division 3 coach preaches to his players is choosing excellence over success as the end goal.

WHY IT MATTERS. After sitting through his recruitment pitch to my son Kelvin, the coach's case for excellence over success stuck with me because it's something we can actually control.

I was only vaguely aware of Messiah before coaches reached out to Kelvin. Turns out, the excellence-over-success philosophy produces, well, a lot of success.

McCarty's record over thirteen years at Messiah is 266–19–18—the second-highest winning percentage in NCAA men's or women's soccer, across all three divisions.

Think of excellence versus success through the prism of business, particularly sales. You could work your ass off to have the best sales pitch, selling the best product, with the best attitude and intent, and . . . fail.

Closing the deal would equal success. So by that measure, you flopped. But maybe the client was broke or the market tanked. Maybe the failure was totally out of your control.

Yet if your pursuit is excellence in your craft, you'll likely win over the long term, even if you endure some inevitable losses in the moment.

Here's why that applies more broadly to your work:

☛ **EXCELLENCE IS HEALTHIER.** Success can create perverse incentives. If being seen as a success is your motivator, you're less likely to obsess about the small details of how and why. You're also less likely to do the right things for the right reasons.

☛ **EXCELLENCE IS REALER.** You could do a mediocre job and still find astonishing success. Maybe you lucked into an easy win or surfed a boom market. But when your luck runs dry or the market crashes, you are . . . still mediocre.

☛ **EXCELLENCE IS ACHIEVABLE.** We control whether we work and think a little smarter each day and push ourselves a little harder. We can sharpen our craft, our character, our performance. Nothing is more satisfying than knowing you're a little better today than you were yesterday. You make *you* your measurement—not someone else's definition of success.

☛ **EXCELLENCE PRODUCES BETTER RESULTS**. Success is fleeting. Excellence lasts—and builds on its momentum. The more you push yourself to up your game, the better you get. The better you get, the more excellent you'll want to be.

CHAPTER 15

BE GOLDILOCKS

I had one speed when we launched *Politico* fifteen years ago: fast and furious.

I wanted everyone to be, well, me—a workaholic who woke up at four a.m. ready to brawl. A small faction of us at *Politico* was like a pack of ravenous wolves hunting for journalistic meat. While our competitors slept, we started mass-producing newsletters and scoops to pop at six a.m., just as Washington insiders were rising.

Our rallying cry everyday was "Win the Morning!" We aimed to "drive the conversation" from the moment people turned on their computer or phone. This was still the era of newspapers and daily, not hourly, news cycles. We exploited the hell out of the slow habits of others. We pushed reporters to break news the second they got it—and then shout it with bold headlines online and timely appearances on cable TV. It was pure metabolism, unrestrained. And it was intoxicating to me. But soul-crushing for many others.

What was terrific for muscling a new brand into existence was terrible for retaining talent. Soon we were haunted by a reputation for being a sweatshop with an untenable burnout rate. Most people simply aren't wired to bound out of bed and sprint until they collapse.

WHY IT MATTERS. One speed for all circumstances is a crazy, reckless way to drive through life. We all need to teach ourselves to swerve away from running too hot or too cold, too often.

A little too hot or too cold is healthy: The extreme highs and lows can sharpen us and open our minds to new ideas and emotions.

But we make our worst, impulsive, foggy decisions when our emotional rpms are redlining. This is true in leadership, at work, and in relationships.

It took me forty years to realize it—and the past decade to truly put it into practice.

Instead, modulate—and moderate—your reactions in tense times. Here's how:

- ☛ **BE AWARE.** Do a self-inventory of how you respond when stress or good times hit. Do you freak out or yell in bad moments? Do you suffer delusions of grandeur in good ones?

- ☛ **KNOW THYSELF.** Identify your triggers. In past jobs, I'd tend to lose it when people acted in a dishonest or lazy way. On the other hand, when someone shone at one thing, I tended to assume they'd rock at everything. In both cases, I've worked on calibrating my response by not getting too cold when people miss the mark or too hot when they nail one specific thing.

☞ **TAME THYSELF.** You can't just muscle yourself into self-control or growth. You need to know specific things that give you calm or clarity. Mine are a mix of faith, meditation, daily exercise, and self-appraisal.

☞ **PRACTICE GOOD-TIMES PARANOIA.** This is particularly true in leadership—temper your optimism or self-love when things are rocking. Realize some of it is luck or good timing. Enjoy the moment, but be a little paranoid about how it happened—or how long it can last.

☞ **PRACTICE BAD-TIMES OPTIMISM.** You learn the most about yourself and others when things go to crap. In the mud of life is where character blooms. So when a bad moment hits, see it as a great learning moment.

THE BOTTOM LINE. Tiny fixes add up to big change.

CHAPTER 16

SELFLESS SUPERSTARS

We have a name at Axios for the ideal employees: selfless superstars.

The aspiration is to find wildly talented and ambitious people (superstars) who put others and the company first (selfless).

WHY IT MATTERS. You need to be ruthless in pursuit of *both* attributes. No leader, no company, no idea will thrive with mediocre or self-absorbed talent.

Selfless superstars are the people who do extraordinary things when things are cooking—and show extraordinary grace when they go to shit.

There are some tricks for spotting and keeping these people.

- ☛ **HUNT RELENTLESSLY.** There are really only two things I screen for when hiring people: Does this person aspire to be the very best at their craft (and is there evidence they're not delusional about achieving it)? And is this person humble enough to put the mission or team above their own selfish ambition?

☛ **DEMAND EXCELLENCE.** Don't be a leader if you can't set a very high threshold and respond if people don't hit it. It is not heartless to insist on excellence. In fact, super-high performers will leave you if they are not surrounded by similarly talented people.

☛ **DEMAND HUMILITY.** Among the most regrettable mistakes I have made in my career was waiting too long to get rid of bad people. At *Politico,* I allowed my admiration of some leaders' intellect to justify their meanness and narcissism. Others are watching and judging whether you live your words.

☛ **FIRE JERKS.** When we started Axios, I would hop onstage and say if I ever saw someone talking behind a colleague's back or tearing someone down to get ahead, they would be "dead to me and never recover." So it was imperative we let go of people who did this. And we did, even when they were insanely talented. Do the same.

☛ **SPOIL YOUR SUPERSTARS.** One true selfless superstar is worth ten or twenty middling performers. Spot these people. And spoil them with thanks, attention, and money.

CHAPTER 17

BE LIKE KATHLEEN

Kathleen Nisbet Halpin, an early Axios hire who made herself indispensable with sharp instincts and good cheer, took to Twitter one morning with wise advice for all the young people in our lives.

It boils down to: Get shit done, no matter how small or dull. Then ask for more—lots more.

WHY IT MATTERS. The fastest way to success isn't sucking up or leaning on a fancy degree. It's doing—and therefore learning—more than your peers, cheerfully and relentlessly.

"I learned what people were working on and looked for ways to help," Kathleen writes. "Practically, this meant taking notes in every meeting and offering to take action items off people's plates. I absorbed everything I could."

Kathleen rose fast in her early twenties to director of strategy—because she knew more, did more, and asked for more than most others.

Not too shabby for an international affairs student with zero business experience.

She left us to get her MBA at New York University to prep for her next big act.

In her words, and through my observations of Kathleen in action, here's a clear road map for any young person to follow:

☛ **PAST IS PAST.** At work, especially in your early days, no one cares about where you came from: what matters most is what you do today and tomorrow. In the trenches, people want to see you deliver the goods with humility and grace. The more you do well, the more you are given.

☛ **VOLUNTEER.** Raise your hand for every little task. Someone needs notes typed up or researched? Do it. Someone looking for help on a project? Offer it. "My biggest piece of advice: The more people associate you with getting things done, the more top of mind you'll be for the next big task," Kathleen said.

☛ **HUSTLE AND LEARN.** Don't just do a lot. Learn a lot. Study what's happening and why. Ask questions. Watch and take notes on people you admire. Also, watch and take notes on the jerks, so you don't become one. "I kept a list of all the words used in meetings that I didn't know and googled them after. I'm not embarrassed to admit in the early days, I searched 'what is B2B?' (a few times 😀)," Kathleen recalled.

THE BOTTOM LINE, VIA KATHLEEN. "Always take the initiative. If you love the company, the mission, and the people, it won't feel like 'work' at all."

CHAPTER 18

NAILING AUDITIONS

An experienced candidate for a top editing job—meeting with Mike Allen, easily our best-known journalist, for the final round—offered a master class in how to bomb an audition.

He clearly took no time to read up on our company, or Mike, or our culture.

Instead, he fixated on his "brand," his power, not the job or how or why he could crush it. He seemed incurious about the job he took time to pursue.

WHY IT MATTERS. Don't be THAT guy. If you're going to take the time to pitch yourself for a new gig, you better really want it—and come ready to dazzle.

Yes, the interviewer also should be selling *you*—top talent is always scarce. But here are a few common traps people fall into, along with a window into what interviewers are listening for:

- ☛ **DON'T BE DULL.** You want to show from the get-go that you'd be an inspiring and sharp colleague. So have an interesting observation about trends relating to the position you're interviewing for. It's like any human conversation: If you leave the interviewer with one smart thing to remember, you've set yourself apart from 99 percent of the competition.

☛ **DON'T BE INCURIOUS.** Ask something specific about how the interviewer's organization is navigating disruption in their sector. (Every sector is being disrupted!) Don't pry: Just show you're fluent in what the interviewer worries about. If they ask you if you have questions, take 'em up on it: "I'm looking forward to getting to know what's on your mind. But there are a couple of things I'm curious about . . ."

☛ **KNOW WHOM YOU'RE TALKING TO.** There's no excuse for not knowing the interviewer's background and claim to fame. Find out their alma mater, hometown, and out-of-work passions—there's almost always a point of connection. Google them. Check their LinkedIn. Don't waste time on chitchat. But a quick mention at the top gets their attention on *you* instead of their last meeting.

☛ **NEVER BAD-MOUTH YOUR CURRENT EMPLOYER.** That's *always* a red flag, and often fatal to your chances. The interviewer doesn't want their organization to be your *next* target. Keep it classy.

☛ **DON'T BABBLE.** Respond in a conversational, substantive way—then stop. If they want more, they'll tell ya.

☞ **THINK BIGGER.** One of the great qualities of up-and-coming generations is that they care more about *values* than their parents did. So if the interviewer doesn't bring up culture and mission, *you* should. If they don't have a good answer, that's helpful information. If *you* don't ask, that could be a strike against you.

☞ **DIG DEEPER.** Don't leave the conversation fuzzy about the job or what crushing it would look like. Asking them what *they* want from the role gets past the formalities and nudges the person to articulate what they *really* want or need. It also shows you think beyond the surface.

☞ **BE PRECISE.** Think about the specific reasons you can rock this job. Write it down in advance. And, without bravado or hyperbole, leave them knowing with precision why you are a potential home-run hire.

THE BOTTOM LINE. If you've gotten to the interview phase, you probably have the skills and experience needed for the job. Now the prospective employer is trying to figure out what you'd be like as a colleague and whether you can make them—and their company—better.

CHAPTER 19

MASTER MENTEE

When I was trying to recruit her away from the *Washington Post* to run sales for Axios, Jacquelyn Cameron had a blunt request. She wanted me to teach her to be a CEO.

WHY IT MATTERS. Jacquelyn's direct ask—"Hey, help me do your job!"—launched some of the most productive monthly mentoring sessions of my life.

We meet at least once a month—often over Zoom, sometimes in person. We waste little time with small talk, other than gossip about media competitors. We dig deep into the engineering of Axios and media operations.

The success of these sessions got me thinking about what makes a great mentee. How could I have confiscated more from willing mentors when I was young and finding my way?

It's simply wanting a "connection" or a closer relationship with someone with power or success. It's not checking the box of merely seeking mentorship or advice, either.

Think of it in terms of working out. Just going to the gym is useless. Going to the gym and half-assing it is useless, too. But if you go to the gym, know your goals, and work your tail off to achieve them, it's magically transformative.

Use Jacquelyn as a template for being a Master Mentee:

- ☛ **HUNGER.** Jacquelyn had a remarkable career before taking this gig, shining at the *New York Times*, *Politico*, and the *Post*. But she was adamant during our recruitment process about wanting to be smarter, better, and even more successful. Her boss, Axios chief business officer Fabricio Drumond, is an ideas machine, and she feeds off it, always craving more. She takes a long view of her career arc.

- ☛ **PURPOSE.** She knows what she wants: to be CEO one day. Love the confidence. Love the specific purpose more. It is so much easier to mentor someone who cuts the BS and just admits to being ambitious. Then as a mentor, you know with precision how to help and steer discussions.

- ☛ **SELF-AWARENESS.** A lot of people who aspire to bigger jobs think they're ready now. She doesn't. Jacquelyn knows her strengths are sales leadership, talent-spotting, and relentless effort. She comes to every session armed with very specific questions beyond her daily duties and current core strengths.

- ☛ **SELF-CONFIDENCE.** She craves direct feedback about areas of weakness. This is where most mentees fail.

They say they want blunt, even brutally honest, feedback—only to turn defensive or deflated when it's given. Jacquelyn lights up—and soaks it in.

☛ **ACTION.** I'm ruthless with my time. Deep down, most mentors want to see a real return on their time investment. Jacquelyn scribbles notes, works concepts into her rap with her direct reports, and puts new ideas into practice. She often comes back to previous conversations for more specifics, more direction. That's a great ROI to me.

THE BOTTOM LINE. To mentees: Never underestimate the power of learning things you struggle with—or aspire to one day master.

CHAPTER 20

WHEN SHIT HAPPENS, SHINE

Two very different but related stories:

STORY 1. In late 2016, Duncan Evans, Robert Allbritton's consigliere and financial adviser, pulled Roy Schwartz, then *Politico*'s chief revenue officer, into his office. Evans told him it was clear I was leaving the company and suggested making Roy CEO with a lucrative salary—IF he kept the deal hidden from me.

Schwartz, an ambitious guy who was eager to make more money to help his family here and in Israel, said that not only was the answer a hard no but that he planned to call me and tell me about the shady plan. He did.

Our friendship and loyalty have been ironclad ever since. Roy went on to cofound Axios and now is CEO of our AI spin-off, Axios HQ.

STORY 2. In 2021, my son James, a terrific athlete with hopes of playing Division 1 college soccer, suffered a season-ending injury in his first game of the season.

This was a bigger-than-normal gut punch—he had missed

most of the previous season with fractures of the small bones around his knee. He was devastated, spent a few hours in despair . . . and then hit the gym the next morning . . . and every morning after . . . to fight back.

He could have wilted. Instead, he worked.

By August of 2022, he had multiple offers and chose High Point University, a rising D1 powerhouse in North Carolina. The coach offered him a spot on their roster, citing his toughness.

WHY IT MATTERS. One of my favorite and fundamental mantras is: When shit happens, shine.

The idea is simple. Anyone can be—or do—good when it's easy. Real character is carved in terrible or tumultuous times.

Roy and James did the hard thing—and only later saw the fruits of shining instead of buckling. We can choose to shine, just like we can choose to whine. It's an active choice.

Seize the moment. There's that memorable line in *Miracle,* the movie about the 1980 U.S. hockey team upsetting the Soviets: "Great moments are born from great opportunity."

You don't confront character-shaping moments every day. But when you do, use them like Roy and James did to do the right, hard thing.

☛ **TAKE RISKS.** Too often we duck from the tough stuff or hide in our fears. But courage is contagious—and lurks inside even the timidest.

With each tough decision, the next one gets a little easier. Soon your natural impulse is to do the right thing—despite the difficulty.

☛ **INSPIRE OTHERS.** Never underestimate the power of a good example. Look how the Roy and James stories live so vividly in my mind years later.

We're all, in some respects, copycats—so give others good stuff to copy. I think about this every time I make a tough call at Axios: Will my words and body language encourage others to respond with calm and class?

☛ **BUILD CHARACTER.** Every day we should be a little better than the one before. None of us goes instantly from slacker to sainthood. We *evolve*, slowly and imperfectly. But the biggest growth spurts come when we handle defining moments with grace and smarts.

THE BOTTOM LINE. Nailing the moments that matter most isn't a shabby aspiration—or legacy.

CHAPTER 21

PLAY POKER

Most of what I know as CEO, I learned from being a reporter. And most of what I know about reporting, I learned from . . . playing poker.

WHY IT MATTERS. I don't toss around a lot of unconventional or controversial parenting advice—*other than* encouraging kids to gamble with real humans . . . for real money . . . at real poker tables.

Disclaimer. Many do not condone or encourage illegal underage betting.

But I do! Okay, I'm talking about playing for mere pennies if you're young or on a tight budget.

The poker table is a classroom filled with invaluable life lessons—and opportunities.

My dad taught me to play at a very early age. I played a lot in college and turned my hobby into a sourcing hook when I hit Capitol Hill as a young reporter.

Turns out, members of Congress and their staff love to gamble—especially at night, especially after voting, and especially after and while drinking. We would sneak away to a member's office, often House majority whip Tom DeLay's leadership office, and play deep into the night.

Some of my best sources were won in those games.

One night at a Republican retreat in Williamsburg, Virginia, I was playing with staff and members of the New York congressional delegation. This hot, fiercely intelligent blonde wanders in and sits next to me. We banter to the point of distraction. A few weeks later, we're dating. One year later, we're engaged. Twenty-two years later, we're still married.

I can't promise you poker will bring you a spouse or even immediate professional benefits. But you will . . .

- **LEARN TO READ PEOPLE.**

    "Show me your eyes, and you may as well show me your cards."

    —*Doyle Brunson, famous poker champ*

    If you sit around a table long enough, you'll start to read people's eyes and twitches, their tendencies and styles, their strengths and weaknesses. Think of poker as a fun way to sharpen your emotional intelligence.

- **LEARN LUCK.**

    "Poker is 100 percent skill and 50 percent luck."

    —*Phil Hellmuth, another famous poker champ*

So much of success flows from getting the right break at the right moment—and being prepared to pounce on it.

Poker shows you how skill can help you win. But only by riding the rhythms of luck can you win big.

· RECOGNIZE FACT PATTERNS.

"Life, like poker, has an element of risk. It shouldn't be avoided. It should be faced."

>*—Edward Norton, actor*

Most people are predictable if you watch closely enough. With time, you can almost anticipate how people will respond in good or bad situations—just like they do with good or bad cards.

And while the fifty-two cards are wildly unpredictable, there is a set number with a concrete hierarchy and a knowable probability of success or failure. Same for most big life decisions with uncertain variables.

· NAVIGATE HIGH PRESSURE.

"Poker is not a team sport. It's every man for himself."

>*—Daniel Negreanu*

There's something about competition, amplified by a few pennies at stake, that messes with your mind. Your blood pressure spikes. Competing impulses race through your head. Instinct grabs hold.

This is most hands of poker—and most tense moments in life. Your brain learns to navigate these moments through trial and error.

- **LEARN TO QUIT.**

"You gotta know when to hold 'em.
Know when to fold 'em."

—Kenny Rogers, "The Gambler"

THE BOTTOM LINE. The biggest mistake poker players make is the same one we all make in relationships, jobs, and bad habits—not knowing when to quit.

Sometimes life deals us bad cards. Sometimes we play good cards poorly. Recognizing your own weaknesses and tendencies helps limit the number of dumb moves you make.

CHAPTER 22

THE ELEVEN COMMANDMENTS

I have hired thousands of people, fired hundreds, and witnessed up close some of the great talents in politics, media, and business.

WHY IT MATTERS. My big takeaway . . . We are a weird-ass species, shaped and then chased (or haunted) forever by our childhood, and motivated and tormented by our need for approval and success.

Basically we are all, deep down, a hot mess. Life is making the most of our mess in a way that yields the deepest, durable satisfaction.

No one teaches us all the small things that help us navigate our mess at work, where we will spend *most* of our waking hours after school and before retirement.

Think of these guiding principles as the Eleven Commandments of Achieving Lasting Satisfaction.

1. **GET PAID FOR DOING SOMETHING YOU LOVE.**
Everything is lighter and easier if you truly enjoy the
thing you spend most of your life doing.

2. **BE THE GOAT.** Strive to be the very best to ever do your
job. You will spend 75 percent of your waking hours
working or thinking about work, so why settle?

3. **SERVE OTHERS.** If it's only about you, you will do the
wrong things for the wrong reasons. Life is empty
alone.

4. **WORK MORALLY.** Honesty, grace, humility, hard work,
and honor are the core values of a work life well lived.

5. **WORK SMART.** Working hard on the wrong or
nonessential things is time wasted. Strive for spending
most of your time on things you do well.

6. **STUDY DEEPLY.** Master the tiny details and panoramic
context of your profession.

7. **STUDY THYSELF.** Be clear-eyed about your gifts and flaws.
It's the only path to betterment.

8. **FORTIFY THYSELF.** Optimal work performance is
impossible without healthy relationships, diet and
exercise, and spirituality and mindfulness.

9. **SAVOR THY WINS.** Take time to celebrate aspirations met.

10. **LEARN FROM LOSS.** The real good stuff often reveals itself in the most painful moments.

11. **FINISH STRONG.** When the clock stops, you want to smile confidently—knowing you did it right and well.

CHAPTER 23

THE WAY TO WIN

In my early years at *Politico*, I was lucky if 25 percent of my hires worked out. Usually I fell for people from prestigious publications with public reputations that did not match their actual talent.

Today, after fifteen years of trial and (lots of) error, I nail about 75 percent. Better—but still imperfect.

WHY IT MATTERS. Hiring people is hard. Some miserable people interview wonderfully. And some wonderful people interview miserably.

Separating the true performers from the posers is an art.

We all want to crush our jobs, get big raises and promotions, and win the approval of peers and bosses. So what makes the best, well, the best?

☞ **EXCEPTIONAL TALENT.** Businesses are not charities. So there is no substitute for uncommonly talented people. You can't teach gifts planted in the womb. But all of us can work relentlessly to be the best at our crafts.

☛ **EXCEPTIONAL WORK ETHIC.** I am all for a work/life balance, in theory. But the most driven are 100 percent self-motivated to do whatever it takes. This is something we all control—and can improve. Most people around me are smarter, but few work harder. With time, this is a massive edge.

☛ **EXCEPTIONAL AMBITION.** You can't teach someone to need to be the very best at what they do. You can model grit and drive, but so much of this dates back to one's genetic predispositions and childhood. This is what motivates you to work harder, rise higher. This ambition usually flows more easily from finding jobs you enjoy so much you would do it for free.

☛ **EXCEPTIONAL GENEROSITY AND HUMILITY.** This might be *the* most important attribute—because self-obsession and arrogance can overshadow and corrupt talent and drive.

☛ **EXCEPTIONAL LOYALTY.** Great companies need great talent. And great talents need great and appreciative companies. Trust sits at the center of this.

CHAPTER 24

BAD APPLES

Most people are good and generous. But some are real, unrepentant, unfixable jerks.

These are the people who poison others or your entire organization with their words or behavior. They usually start small, with off-putting comments or actions, and then reveal themselves in full with repeated refusals to apologize or change.

WHY IT MATTERS. A good hack for work is to study the jerks—the people who do the wrong things for the wrong reasons. Then do the opposite. And purge them from your life if possible.

It's easy to be inspired by acts of great heroism or actions. But many of my defining memories come from witnessing baffling or bad human behavior.

It's easy to get paralyzed by stewing about people cutting corners or acting like asses. Study them instead.

You can shape your own style by trying never to do what drives you most nuts when others do it.

To this day, I am obsessed with candor, honesty, transparency, and high achievement, because I witnessed other leaders reward indirection, dishonesty, secrecy, and blind loyalty over merit.

At Axios, I took it several steps further, making it a de facto fireable offense if people routinely were self-centered, petty, or mean. In making this clear in words and actions, we have mostly eliminated the mischief-making and backbiting all of us witness and hate at school, at work, and in relationships.

Here are the most searing lessons I have learned from watching bad people who do bad things:

☞ **BADNESS TRICKLES DOWN—FAST.** Any bad habit in a group or company can be traced to someone at the very top. You see this at schools, on jobs, and on sports teams.

☞ **BAD HABITS ARE INSANELY CONTAGIOUS.** One reason we prohibit people at Axios from talking crap about colleagues is witnessing how free others then feel to do the same.

☞ **BEHIND MOST BAD BEHAVIOR LURKS DEEP INSECURITY.** Beware of those who surround themselves with people with bad characters or limited talent. Bad people like to be around people who share—or tolerate—their bad values. Or they gravitate toward people who enable them with their silence or compliance. They hate being around secure people who point out their shortcomings.

☛ **DON'T BE DELUSIONAL ABOUT OUR SPECIES.** It is so tempting to try to see a path for someone who is routinely selfish or petty or untrustworthy to change. Most fully formed humans don't. Run.

☛ **WE ALL NEED A DJ.** A longtime colleague, Danielle Jones, has a sixth sense for spotting bad apples. And she isn't shy about holding us accountable. Find people like her who have high character and trust—and listen to them.

DJ recently left Axios to return to *Politico* but left her mark as our talent whisperer and the heart and soul of our company. These are the tells she looks for in spotting problematic people:

- Lack of humility.
- Lack of authenticity.
- Favoring personal ambition over the greater good.
- Taking yourself too seriously.

THE BOTTOM LINE. Good bosses, company, and friends are everywhere. Live life in perpetual pursuit of them. Purge the others.

PART 3

CHAPTER 25

JUST LEAD

I was a late-blooming leader.

I never led any team on anything until the summer of 2006, when at thirty-five, I pushed and pulled a small group of journalists to start *Politico.*

Len Downie, then the executive editor of the *Washington Post,* reacted with a mix of oh-isn't-this-cute bemusement and WTF bafflement when I explained my plans to bolt the *Post* to help lead a new company. "You've never even asked to edit a story or manage a few people," he said. "Now you're going to run a company?"

WHY IT MATTERS. In the next five years, I transformed myself from an aloof, lone-wolf, never-ran-crap journalist to a confident, can-do, if flawed leader of hundreds. I learned to lead by screwing up a lot, self-correcting, watching others around me do it terribly, and studying those outside of *Politico* getting it right.

Being a journalist helped a lot. This provided a front-row seat to powerful leaders across America, and easy access to call or meet with people worth copying.

Sure, I read a lot of leadership books—Jim Collins's *Good to*

Great, Jack Welch's *Jack: Straight from the Gut,* Al Neuharth's *Confessions of an S.O.B.* Truth is, most business books capture at best one or two new ideas or tactics. So they were only marginally helpful.

The best way to learn to lead is to build a core belief framework—and then just do it. With time, you learn by leading—and constantly adjusting and hopefully evolving.

There is a big difference between leading and management. Think of leadership as smart ideas and persuasive inspiration; management as turning this into tactics and action.

As I think back, my belief system and style are a pick-and-choose mix of several people I met along the way:

- The self-confident speaking style of JPMorgan Chase CEO Jamie Dimon.

- The serve-others-first humility of Mike Allen.

- The don't-flinch, fight-for-others spunk of Autumn.

- The contagious swagger of the late *Washington Post* executive editor Ben Bradlee.

- The equally contagious optimism of Watts of Love founder Nancy Economou.

- The confident enthusiasm for—and belief in—workplace culture of Edelman president Lisa Ross.

- The people-matter-most heart of Axios chief of staff Kayla Brown.

- The small-details-matter perfectionism of David Rogers.

- The fierce obsession with lifelong self-betterment of Ariana Huffington.

- The insistence on work ethic and honesty of my father, John VandeHei.

There are countless ways to lead and be a worthy leader. But the following things strike me as indispensable:

☛ **A MORAL FRAMEWORK.** You can be immoral and lead people . . . to dark places, fear, and evil. Leadership is a precious gift, the rare chance to bring others success, meaning, courage, and joy. Take this as seriously as parenting. You need to anchor firmly to values others should and will emulate. The non-negotiable morals are honesty, integrity, an appetite or willingness to do the hard thing when it's unpopular, and some level of humility. If this is not you, please don't lead.

☛ **A PROBING MIND.** A very curious mind is table stakes for leading. You can get away with incurious and static thinking as a manager. Leading demands constant reading, watching, studying, and questioning yourself. You are looking for what others can't see—and gazing deep into the future simultaneously.

☞ **COURAGE.** Anyone can make simple decisions with scant consequences. But leaders must be willing, even eager, to do tough, uncertain, sometimes painful, and wildly unpopular things. Pleasing people cannot be what drives you. Nor can avoiding embarrassment or mistakes. You need to be willing to be unpopular—or wrong.

☞ **RELENTLESSNESS.** You should not ask others to work harder, think smarter, dig deeper than you do. Leadership is not a forty-hour gig. It's an all-the-time one. You need to constantly sharpen your mind, body, and morality so you can pull others along as much with your actions as words. The honor of leading comes loaded with much responsibility.

☞ **CANDOR.** People often listen for what they want to hear—so ambiguity is deafening. This is what causes confusion, resentment, and wasted time. Only with honest, direct clarity can you break through and guide people to new places. Self-candor is equally important: You need to develop the capacity to be blunt with yourself to spot and correct shortcomings.

☞ **GRIT.** Get used to failing and frustration, daily. Leading is not winning applause onstage. It's dealing with the weird shit our weird species does every day. It's also dealing with bad hires, terrible decisions, unpopular products, missed budgets, and controversy. You need to be okay with getting kicked in the gut and smiling on that stage the next day.

☞ **AGILITY.** Every dimension of work changes faster than most humans can handle. This demands faster-than-others-can adaptation—the ability to tweak your views, style, and strategy on the fly. And then the ability to take others along.

CHAPTER 26

SOFT POWER

My first crack at leadership, in the garage-band days of starting *Politico*, was often a disaster: I had two speeds—fast and faster—and it drove others nuts and off the road.

No wonder we soon had a reputation as a sweatshop with a high burnout rate.

WHY IT MATTERS. Since then a revolution has unfolded, with soft power replacing hard power, EQ trumping IQ, purpose rivaling profit. It is upending how everyone leads—including me.

You simply cannot be a leader at any level for very long if you don't adapt to these new realities with a soft-power mentality.

I was a political reporter—self-absorbed, as reporters are—when I quit the *Washington Post* in 2006 to start *Politico*. We turned an on-the-fly idea into a valuable company with five hundred people, including reporters around the world.

My "business school" was screwing up. The first time I had to let someone go, I humiliated the guy, totally botching it. I hired only people wired like me and rolled my eyes about "culture" and "process" and "work/life balance." It was all action, little thought.

We did the impossible, but the pace and style was untenable and unscalable. It became clear when good people left complaining of exhaustion and every recruit asked about our boys' club, sweatshop reputation that we needed to change.

So using my journalistic tricks and tools, I became a student of what works, what motivates people, and how to get the best from them.

Ten years after launching *Politico*, we started Axios. Five years later, our team is four hundred plus. I took everything I'd learned by doing it wrong—and turned it toward building a company that has tons of ambition and insists on excellence, but with humanity cooked in.

Here are my biggest discoveries that will help you think about deploying soft power in life and leadership:

- ☛ **BE A SELFLESS SUPERSTAR.** There's no substitute for talent. But you'll hit a low ceiling fast if you're not humble enough to put others before yourself. This allows you to fuse doing good work with doing good, period.

- ☛ **DITCH JERKS FAST.** This is true in life and business: Self-centered, egotistical asses are cancerous. Cut 'em out before their badness spreads—and infects you. People won't trust you—or do the best work—if they think you're subjecting them to needless torment.

☛ **CLARITY RULES.** Quit being indirect. So many people dance around hard discussions out of fear or insecurity. This is time wasted. There's magic in polite, direct, transparent conversations. Try it. You will get better with each attempt.

☛ **ONLY HIRE CAUSE-FIRST STARS.** You want unapologetically ambitious and high-achieving people who can put the cause or the company first. They are gems. Do everything you can to spoil them—and thank them.

☛ **SHARE.** There is a special magic in transparency about your views, moves, strategy, and decision-making. It eradicates suspicion fast. You hold a position of power. So use it for good.

THE BOTTOM LINE. If you try to lead today with a *Mad Men* mentality or work at a company run like that . . . stop.

CHAPTER 27

DON'T NIBBLE

One of my favorite maxims from one of my favorite business books is: "If you are going to eat shit, don't nibble."

WHY IT MATTERS. Ben Horowitz, writing in *The Hard Thing About Hard Things*, coined this wonderful, if crude, precept for taming the human instinct to avoid tough actions. He was spot-on.

Think of all the time wasted avoiding tough conversations or difficult decisions or unpleasant moments. We dither, ignore, nibble around the edges.

All this does is prolong misery for you—and everyone else involved.

Consider all the areas we nibble instead of chomp at work:

- ☛ **TAKING BLAME.** Many think it shows weakness, but owning up to a boneheaded move quickly and emphatically shows confidence—and puts the matter behind you faster.

- ☛ **APOLOGIZING.** Think of all the times you dragged your feet or said sorry in small, incremental ways. A fast, full-throated apology is the only effective, timesaving one.

☛ **KILLING BAD IDEAS**. Never underestimate the human capacity to rationalize and keep doing things you know aren't working. No one wants to admit failure. Don't throw good money at bad. You are better off making fast calls and fast adjustments.

☛ **FIRING PEOPLE**. Nowhere do managers nibble more than here. It sucks. It's uncomfortable. But ask any manager and they will tell you their experience shows the moment you think it's not going to work, it won't. Trust your gut and act fast.

☛ **QUITTING**. Think of all the times you dragged your feet on kicking a bad habit or ditching a lame job. Same in leadership: Know when it's time to leave the bar. Then bolt.

THE BOTTOM LINE. This is dangerous advice to offer, but in my experience, the moment you think something is off and unfixable, you're almost always right. Don't spend weeks, months, or years nibbling. Do it in one big bite.

CHAPTER 28

RADIATE OUT

The one novel concept binding the success of both *Politico* and Axios was our "radiate out" theory of power and influence.

WHY IT MATTERS. The idea was simple in construct but highly difficult in practice. Find reporters who could hook the most powerful, difficult readers to reach—the president of the United States at *Politico,* and top CEOs, tech leaders, and White House officials at Axios. Then the tight circle around them would follow, then the larger circle around them as well, and so forth.

Ultimately, you get a huge audience to pay attention because the people they admire, follow, or listen to are reading you.

This is the opposite of how most media companies or leaders think. They shoot for the masses first. To us, this creates perverse incentives to think broadly and dumb down the content.

I still remember the very moment we knew *Politico* hit the bull's-eye of the radiate-out board. It was Valentine's Day, 2007, one month after our launch. President George W. Bush called a press conference, and to our surprise blew *Politico* the sweetest of Valentine kisses. Sitting in the back of the White House East Wing room was Mike Allen, our star reporter.

THE PRESIDENT: Michael. Michael, who do you work for? (*Laughter.*)

MIKE: Mr. President, I work for Politico.com.

THE PRESIDENT: Pardon me? Politico.com?

MIKE: Yes, sir. Today. (*Laughter.*)

THE PRESIDENT: You want a moment to explain to the American people exactly what—(*Laughter.*)

MIKE: Mr. President, thank you for the question. (*Laughter.*)

THE PRESIDENT: Quit being so evasive.

NBC'S DAVID GREGORY: You should read it.

THE PRESIDENT: Is it good? You like it?

THE PRESIDENT: David Gregory likes it. I can see the making of a testimonial. (*Laughter.*)

Here we were, one month old, unknown to most, and the president was doing a free commercial for us. Our Rosslyn office rocked like a stadium at the Super Bowl.

But this was not by accident. We had hired reporters we knew could turn the heads of the most powerful. And we told them very specifically: "Tape a picture of Nancy Pelosi or the

White House chief of staff on your computer: THEY are your audience."

This same theory worked for Axios. We wanted tech and private equity people to read us, so we hired Dan Primack, easily the smartest and most wired in reporter in that space. We wanted media executives to read us, so we hired Sara Fischer, easily the smartest and most wired in reporter in her space. The results were magical.

This concept works outside of media and offers any aspiring leader a novel edge.

- ☞ **FOCUSING YOUR TIME.** I'm constantly doing an inventory of the *few* big things I do better than others that ripple through our company with the largest impact. This allows me to influence the largest number of people most efficiently. And avoid trying to do so many things that I do nothing.

- ☞ **AMPLIFYING YOUR VALUES.** You cannot get large groups of people to emulate dozens of values important to you. Pick a few that can echo loudly and broadly enough to shape things in your image. For me, it's straight-shooting candor, humility, and high achievement. I look for ways to ideally show or tell about each week so they take root and spread.

- ☞ **DESIGNING PRODUCTS.** It's easy to get lost thinking of millions of customers. Instead, focus on ONE core buyer or user, the ideal consumer: if that person likes it, others will, too. Maybe find that actual individual and bounce early iterations off them. We sometimes do this with tiny focus groups of a few. Either way, it sharpens your focus.

☞ **ALIGNING YOUR TEAM.** What are the two or three things your direct reports must do to radiate success throughout the organization? Write each one down, condensed into one clear, crisp sentence, then share it in writing and meetings weekly. It's remarkable how quickly others will repeat your language and amplify your focus.

☞ **COMMUNICATING.** This is where most leaders go off the rails. They are either so long-winded they hide what's important in a torrent of words, or so tentative they obscure it in foggy corporate babbling. Here, too, always whittle down your thinking to at most three ideas in three sentences each, so you have the best chance of spreading your message.

CHAPTER 29

RADICAL TRANSPARENCY

I watched so many people at so many companies I worked for gossip about what they thought the bosses were scheming or thinking. They wasted countless hours—and stirred endless drama—trying to read body language or cryptic messages for hints about company finances, strategy, or decision-making.

So when we started Axios, we were hell-bent on purging the wondering and whispering that happens when people feel blind to what's REALLY happening.

Our solution was radical transparency: Share everything with everybody often so everyone feels in the loop and included.

WHY IT MATTERS. By sharing everything other than how much someone makes or why someone left—those exceptions are out of respect for the individual—we mostly eliminated the suspicion and resentment that flows so easily from not knowing what's really going on.

We also treat people like reasonable adults and simply ask

others to do the same. A funny thing happens when you trust people with sensitive information: they appreciate it and keep it in the family.

This has helped create a more dynamic, trusting culture at Axios.

Before we started Axios, four of us—Mike Allen, Roy Schwartz, Kayla Brown, and I—spent countless hours reflecting on our time at *Politico* and dreaming up the ideal culture for an as-yet-unnamed company.

We wanted to work with insanely talented people, but also insanely good people, in a wildly ambitious but truly enjoyable workplace.

To do this, we knew we would need to be intolerant of jackasses and mischief-makers, but also come up with mechanisms to spread trust.

A key component was treating adults like adults and trusting them with sensitive information and nuance. Our theory was that it's hard to be suspicious or feel left out if you see your bosses being trusting and transparent.

Here are three things we do that might be helpful in other settings:

- ☛ **OVERSHARE.** In relationships, at work, as leaders, you build trust by being open and honest, constantly and consistently. You cannot simply say you are transparent; you demonstrate it with hundreds of little acts of openness. At Axios, we write a weekly newsletter to all staff with a candid, behind-the-curtain look at what we are doing and why. It is written by a human (me and Kayla) in our voice with no corporate-crap language.

☞ **TAKE TOUGH QUESTIONS.** One of the hardest but best things we do is take questions every Monday, read them verbatim even if it hurts, and answer forthrightly and non-defensively.

Make no mistake; this can be hard. We went through a short season a few years back where a few people wrote in questions aimed at rattling me. An example: "How can a straight, white, cisgender guy like you make decisions for all of us?" My response was simple: "Yes, I am a straight, married white dude, but I use transparent forums like this to better understand people with different realities than mine."

Some execs wanted to stop the practice because it was uncomfortable. But we did not—and hopefully it showed we were transparent even when it was hard.

Truth is, this is like a pressure release valve, slowly untwisted. It lets people vent in tiny bursts instead of bottling it up and exploding.

☞ **ASK TOUGH QUESTIONS.** People need to know with total clarity what you want to know—and why. It's human nature to sugarcoat the inquiry if it's sensitive or second-guessing. Don't. Most people will hide in the gray or hear what THEY want to hear. Leave no room to doubt what and why you are asking.

Resist retreat. Twice, someone on staff leaked private

Axios discussions, presumably to embarrass me or a colleague or stir up trouble. My initial reaction was annoyance—and then a fleeting thought that we needed to stop being so transparent.

But then I realized the good of thousands of open conversations far outweighs the bad of two conversations leaked.

THE BOTTOM LINE. It's true in work and life: Demystifying things with candor and transparency eliminates a lot of the needless drama and sneaky, toxic suspicion.

CHAPTER 30

FIRING WITH DIGNITY

The first time I fired someone, it was a debacle.

WHY IT MATTERS. I was as subtle as a sledgehammer. My lack of finesse—and dignity in delivery—got me an F.

It was early 2007. John Harris, one of our *Politico* cofounders, and I decided we had to let one of our early employees go.

We called the guy in, and I recited all the things he was bad at—and told him he was canned. I was candid but candidly cold and a jerk. The poor guy never saw it coming.

Afterward, Harris turned to me and said, "Um, I will handle the firing thing from now on."

We weren't wrong about the guy's performance. But we were wrong about how we handled it. With time, I radically reshaped how I thought about letting people go.

First, the obvious: No one wants to fire or be fired. It sucks.

But here's a cold, hard truth about running a business: You sometimes hire the wrong person for the wrong job at the wrong time.

You need to act the moment you realize it can't be corrected. Otherwise, your company or team will suffer and stagnate.

One of the biggest mistakes managers make is rationalizing not making the hard but correct move. The moment you think you should fire someone, chances are you should do it ASAP.

There are ways to do this with grace and class:

- ☛ **NO SURPRISES.** By the time someone comes into a meeting to be fired, it should be clear to all what's about to happen and why. This is where candor matters most. If you're giving or getting unvarnished feedback—and clear instructions on what needs to improve and on what timeline—the end should be obvious to all.

- ☛ **DON'T WAIT.** So many people duck hard, uncomfortable discussions. It's a terrible way to treat people. Anyone who isn't living up to expectations should know with total precision why—and what they must do to improve.

- ☛ **BE GRACIOUS.** Most people don't get fired for stealing or scandal. It's usually not the right fit or the right season of life for the company or individual. Be clear and direct, but don't overexplain or get dragged into a point-by-point debate.

- ☛ **BE CLASSY.** One trick for easing the pain—and stain—of getting fired is giving the person time to leave on their own and find another job from a position of strength. Getting fired is awful, but it can also be an opportunity to listen, learn, and self-correct. We often let people stay on the payroll for a few months to make it appear that they are simply looking for something better, not out of work and scrambling for employment.

THE BOTTOM LINE. Now that we practice this approach, we've had people later thank us for letting them go, and how it was handled.

CHAPTER 31

THE ROY RULE

Roy Schwartz, Axios cofounder and president, has a provocative hiring rule: Always go for people who want—and could do—your job.

WHY IT MATTERS. Too many managers hire too defensively—they want to protect their own gig while not getting overshadowed by dazzling talent below.

Or they hire too passively—they simply want butts in seats to be able to check off their list. This is why so many institutions grow complacent or rot.

Roy worked as a management consultant at Gallup before joining us. He was a student of Gallup's treasure trove of data on why people and individuals crush it—or get crushed.

His ambition is unbridled. But so is his willingness to follow his own rule. He has a terrific nose for limitless talent and happily drafts off their success.

The only way to be a great leader—and to create a great organization—is to have the self-confidence to hire people who might be better and shine brighter than you from the get-go.

THIS APPLIES MORE BROADLY TO LIFE. Too often, we fear being around people who work harder, exercise more frequently, or volunteer more cheerily. It's human nature to want to measure ourselves against people who aren't outpacing us. What better way to look good?!

But here's the secret. The easiest way to get better at something is to surround yourself with people better than you—and learn.

In the workplace, the big winners are self-confident leaders who hire exceptionally motivated and talented staff. Here are five tips for doing just that:

- **EMBRACE AMBITION.** You want people who are hungry, hyper-motivated, hell-bent on being the best at what they do. Look for signs of competitiveness and preparation beyond wishful aspirational talk. Most successful people stack wins on top of wins.

- **IRON SHARPENS IRON.** You will rarely run faster by running with someone slower. In work and life, it takes a mix of confidence and humility to draft off those better, faster, smarter to up your own game. Fear holds us back.

- **NO SUBSTITUTE FOR TALENT.** A great employee will forever be worth a dozen fine ones. This is harsh but true. No need to apologize for hunting relentlessly for them.

- **BEWARE OF I.** One telltale red flag is when people take credit for those previous wins and characterize themselves as the hero. You want people who use *we* a lot and speak persuasively about how they helped tease out others' terrific work.

☛ **PLAY THE LONG GAME.** The moment you decide to get into management or leadership, you rely on others to succeed—and to make you look good. So you need superstar talent. Yes, that might mean their ambition leads them to leave one day. But that simply means your network of success stories grows.

THE BOTTOM LINE. As CEO, I often tell investors and others that our greatest success at Axios has been creating an executive team full of future CEOs.

Many of them probably dream of being the Axios CEO one day—and definitely could be.

CHAPTER 32

WORK ANYWHERE

Gone are the days when we all gathered in one office, for set hours on set days, for in-person meetings and desk-to-desk gossiping.

WHY IT MATTERS. Stop wishing for a world that was and adapt to what is. Any high-performing company needs people working from anywhere because a lot of high-performing people demand it.

I have talked with dozens of CEOs and hundreds of workers about this raging debate.

The CEOs privately say they are convinced that with work from home, productivity dips, culture softens, creativity wanes, and a few but not inconsequential number of employees will get paid to do yoga and chill.

The workers retort: This is nonsense. Most adults are fully capable of working better without time-sucking commutes and noisy, distraction-filled offices. Sure, they might exercise more or take breaks at home, but ultimately that makes them better employees.

I do worry about two big risks of working from anywhere:

- Younger workers benefit more than they realize from being in the trenches in person, grappling with tough, teaching moments. There is a magic in human interaction. How can you learn to be a true leader on Zoom or Slack?

- It is way harder to create strong emotional bonds with colleagues and your company from your couch. People stay in jobs and thrive when they feel tight connections.

Here are four steps Axios takes to mitigate the risk of WFH:

☞ **HIRE SELF-MOTIVATED, DRIVEN PEOPLE.** You need to screen hard for those who naturally blend work with life, motivated by passion for their craft, not money or rules. Clock-punchers or check-cashers are very problematic in a WFH world.

☞ **CREATE NEW HUMAN INTERACTIONS.** We take the money reserved for office space and spend it on company retreats, team off-sites, and regional and local meet-ups. We encourage employees in the same city, regardless of their job, to get together at a bar or for coffee.

☞ **COMMUNICATE UNTIL YOU ANNOY YOURSELF.** A good CEO or manager should be writing to—or Zooming with—their teams at least weekly and ideally more to amplify the purpose, the strategy, the goals, the common pursuit. This is more than most employees ever got when everyone was in person. We created software—called HQ—to do this easily and effectively.

☞ **CREATE NEW PERFORMANCE MEASUREMENTS.** You do need tighter measurement or monitoring to make sure everyone is doing the right thing in the right order at the right speed. The bigger you are, the more important this is. Managers don't see people doing their work, so they need more specific measurements, such as the number of in-person meetings salespeople are conducting or the velocity of actual code produced by each programmer.

THE BOTTOM LINE. Every employee needs to know that with great freedom comes great responsibility. If you work from home, the more you see colleagues in person, the better. The more you connect by something other than text, the better.

My personal view is that if you are lucky enough to live near a physical office, use it. I go in every day I am in town.

If you are not near an office, force yourself to connect with others often and consistently, on the phone or Zoom.

I am big on living in the world we have, not wish we had. The truth is, during the pandemic, people moved away, started new lives and habits, and often had a lot of choices where to work.

It's our job to tap into this and turn it into the best virtual, dispersed workplace ever.

CHAPTER 33

WARTIME LEADERSHIP

I bullied my way into my first gig as CEO at *Politico,* six years after starting it. I forced the owner to make me CEO by threatening to walk.

We were too timid to start the company with venture capital in 2006. Back then, it seemed too risky for us to leave prime jobs and certainly for any reporter from an established publication to take the leap with us. Instead, we chose one rich owner, Robert Allbritton, who gave us minimal shadow equity and smartly demanded full ownership and ultimate control. I spent a sizable chunk of my early years mostly leading our editorial coverage.

But as *Politico* grew, it seemed obvious to me we needed one leader, a CEO—not the group grope of cofounders. And I thought it should be me. I was getting good at leading people and understood the business intimately. My instincts for spotting talent were growing sharper and my appreciation for the corporate culture, deeper.

Robert hated the idea of me moving from editor to CEO,

arguing I was too inexperienced and more maniacal than managerial. It wasn't until I threatened to quit that he caved, reluctantly.

WHY IT MATTERS. Robert and I disagreed on many big issues. But he was right that the Jim of 2009 was built more for battle, not peacetime stewardship, which draws more heavily on steady operational expertise and managing managers.

This tension is true for any aspiring leader: traits that help you quickly build a company or rise to power in chaos don't always translate into leading in calmer times.

Wartime leaders tend to be risk-takers, hands-on doers, fast-acting multitaskers, and live-off-the-land survivalists. Peacetime leaders need to be steady leaders of leaders, process-minded and longer-term thinkers.

Not many people are good at both.

My stint as *Politico* CEO was a success, thanks to a savvy surrounding cast including chief operating officer Kim Kingsley (now of Airbnb), chief revenue officer Roy Schwartz, and many others.

We snapped back into wartime mode when we launched Axios, shifted ever so slightly into peacetime mode after a few years of wins—before cranking back into battle gear when the economy hit turbulence in 2022. Wartime is my happy place.

What wartime-versus-peacetime leadership looks like:

☛ **SURVIVAL > SANITY.** You claw your way through each day or week instead of setting up thoughtful structures and processes that can last a lifetime. Failure is not an option, so you structure your time and thinking to keep things alive and moving. You put some long-term thinking aside until you stabilize. In peacetime, you're focused on the future and the culture, leaders, process, and money to get you there.

☞ **EATING GLASS > BUILDING WINDOWS.** You focus on the must-haves instead of nice-to-haves. Do whatever it takes it to win on the life-and-death decisions. You will break some glass. There will be time to clean it up later. In peacetime, you are building foundations and structures to scale—and to last.

☞ **DOERS > DESIGNERS.** In tough times, you need people who can carry a lot of freight without collapsing. These are the get-shit-done warriors. They can bounce from fire to fire and find ways to put them out. They don't wilt. The smart, credentialed, structured thinking C-suite types are indispensable . . . after you survive and grow. They're systems engineers.

☞ **BRAVADO > REALISM.** You don't have time for rational thought when things go to shit. You need to will the impossible into existence. This takes a mix of bravado, Barnumesque behavior, and charisma to get people to ignore fear and reality. There's a reason Bud Tribble, one of the original members of the Macintosh team, called Apple CEO Steve Jobs's gift for getting programmers to do the impossible his "reality distortion field." In peacetime, reality takes over. You need to build something durable and scalable and not reliant on a few heroic warriors.

☛ **CASUALTIES > CALM.** This is the hardest one to stomach. People often get hurt when companies are fighting for survival. You make quick, tough, imperfect decisions. You often don't have time to get paralyzed about how it makes people feel. You will have time to repent and repair . . . if you survive. Once you start to thrive, you can't keep piling up casualties. People's expectations change. They want more predictability and stability. They want more safety.

CHAPTER 34

SURRENDERING POWER

Kristin Burkhalter was a Division 1 athlete at Duke University and later helped build the Stars Lacrosse Club, one of the most powerful and durable pipelines of high school talent in America.

Today, she's an Axios SVP who oversees events—our fastest-growing business in 2023—as a leader, coach, and doer.

Kristin runs events and creative strategy like a stand-alone business inside a bigger one, with full autonomy and delegated power.

WHY IT MATTERS. Kristin's earning—and our giving her—more authority provides a lens into one of the hardest decisions leaders make: when to delegate power and decision-making.

This is a common complaint among my own team: why won't you delegate more power? And it's a common complaint from my own team's own teams. This is a question that bedevils bosses and ambitious people everywhere.

There's no scientific threshold to clear. But there are some clear markers:

☛ **CRUSH IT.** Power should rarely flow from title or tenure. You earn it. Kristin consistently hit or beat her numbers and, more important, always delivers blue-chip productions. Power shifted naturally to her. She earned it.

☛ **ELIMINATE STRESS.** Any CEO or top executive has an endless pile of crap they need to rescue or fix. The greatest gift you can give us is confidence you can deliver competently, consistently, and drama-free. The highest praise I pay Kristin is that I spend zero time thinking about events.

☛ **WIN TRUST.** I—and her direct boss, Axios chief business officer Fabricio Drumond—trust Kristin to deliver. Why? She didn't ASK for autonomy. She won it, with her actions AND character. It's big things like never screwing up a big Axios production, but also small things like taking personal responsibility for missteps and knowing when to bring complex knots to us to help untie.

☛ **BE HUMBLE.** Harkening back to her sports career, Kristin is terrific at always crediting "her team" and all the other execs who have her back. This makes everyone want to cheer for her and get her back, in return.

☛ **PASS IT ON.** You will get stuck fast if you win delegated power but fail to do the same for others. I am only as good as my executive team. Kristin is only as good as the future coaches she is training. Ebonie Gibbs was an early participant in our future leaders program at Axios, so I got to spend some nice chunks of time mentoring her. She was clearly talented and ambitious. But it was Kristin who quite quickly tossed more power her way. Ebonie is now a VP, a homegrown success.

☞ **DELIVER THE GOODS.** You won't keep delegated power long if you cannot keep proving you earned it. This means getting better and smarter and ringing up more successes every month, quarter, and year. The cold hard truth of power is that it's easier to lose than it is to win. In a tough year for media in 2023, Kristin grew her business 60 percent and expanded into the big, yearly conference business.

CHAPTER 35

WEED WHACKING

My direct reports at Axios threw some very direct feedback at me during our midyear 2023 reviews.

A common theme: "Jim should get the hell out of the weeds and focus on what he does best." It's annoying and trust-sapping, they said. See, we do practice candor!

WHY IT MATTERS. They're right. I am susceptible to one of the biggest problems in the modern workplace: wasting time on things better handled by someone else—or not done at all.

Truth is, I should—and do—know better since I have total visibility into what matters most in growing Axios successfully. I'm also typically ruthless with my time and attention. So it shows the powerful pull of time-sucking distractions.

But most people are foggier about what's most important to the company or cause. This leads to doing things out of habit or confusion. You end up working harder to do less.

So when they hear "work smarter" or "do more with less," they want to punch you in the nose. They feel they're working to exhaustion already. So digging deeper sounds like a mean and unrealistic taunt.

I constantly push myself and the Axios staff to do a work inventory to see how they in fact can do more with less. How can they put that same energy into the things that move the needle more powerfully?

It's striking how often I find people doing things we once cared about but no longer do: "Wait, this was a Jim obsession four years ago!" Or spending lots of time on unimportant tasks: "I thought this was mission-critical!"

This, in turn, keeps them from doing the things that make them shine—and feel better about their performance and their company.

Qian Gao, our chief people officer, has three questions she puts to staff to help focus them on working smarter:

1. What are the things in your job that you least like to do?

2. What would you do if you had one more hour in the week?

3. What do you do that you don't think you need to do?

These questions are designed to get people to focus and trim busywork and then plan more time on what matters most.

You might take it one step deeper and think about your typical week—at work and home—and how you allocate your time to work and live optimally.

- Are you allocating time outside of work for exercising or other activities that help you think clearer and more confidently at work?

- At work, are you allocating most of your energy to things you are authentically very good or great at? This is what drives the most fulfillment for most people. Figure out how to whittle down or lop off the rest.

THE BOTTOM LINE. You should do this wildly clarifying exercise yourself every quarter. You'll be shocked by how easily you can reorient to spending more time on things you are uniquely good at and jazzed by.

CHAPTER 36

THE SIMPLICITY DOCTRINE

Occam's razor teaches that the simplest explanation is usually the right one.

Here's the Axios razor: The simplest way of doing things is usually the right one.

WHY IT MATTERS. Too many people lard up ideas, processes, teams, or companies with needless complexity. Simplicity, by contrast, greases velocity, productivity, and profitability.

This is my big obsession heading into the era of tight labor markets and artificial intelligence. How can we cut away complexity at every level, in every area, to make everything we do simple, fast, intuitive for staff—and readers?

This fights against the human habit of keeping things once we secure them.

At work, that habit is very hard to break.

Think of it this way: Every new person needs to do something and usually wants to add their own special something to it. Each new something breeds new complexities, merely by existing.

Once something exists, it's rarely killed. Or even revisited. Killing things is often harder than creating them—that something has an owner and constituencies. It's easier to justify keeping it than killing it. This is why you don't throw out that shirt you never wear.

This is why everything big becomes bureaucratic. (It's also why public policy is so hard to fix.)

And it's why start-ups lose their juice.

Everyone should do a Simplicity Audit of their life and work. Given the speed of change, do it every three to six months. Ask yourself:

- Do we really need this—or use this often enough to justify it?

- Is there a faster, easier way to do things?

Some ways to think about simplicity:

☛ **MORE IS OFTEN LESS.** There's an inverse relationship between the number of people involved and the quality/velocity of products. Most managers think the opposite. The instinct is to think about adding to fix things, instead of eliminating things you already have.

☛ **SIMPLICITY WORKS EVERYWHERE.** One of the smartest things we did seven years ago was to adopt a principle we call elegant efficiency for all our visual and product designs. Readers yearn for clarity—so you need guardrails to block complexity. The same with our Smart Brevity writing architecture. It's all about making life simpler and more intuitive.

☛ **A SIMPLICITY CZAR.** If I were designing the company from scratch, I'd have a CSO—chief simplicity officer— whose job was to make sure everything we did was constantly reviewed for ease and essentialism. This mandate falls on Axios's new head of operations. But everyone needs this role, in title or focus.

☛ **BACK TO BASICS.** Constantly revisiting what your team or consumers need is the key. Would this exist if we started from scratch today? If not, kill it—or simplify it.

CHAPTER 37

ELEVATE *COMMUNICATIONS*

Every organization in the world—business, nonprofit, or government—needs to rethink, quickly and dramatically, how it communicates with employees, donors, customers, constituents, and shareholders.

WHY IT MATTERS. Communications is now arguably the most important skill for any leader and function inside any organization, big or small. And most suck at it.

Think about running anything since COVID:

- Many people are still working from couches or kitchens or coffee shops—and will never return to a physical office to connect and learn.

- Every person has more notifications, bells, or pings lighting up their phone than ever before. Hence, perpetual distraction.

So people today are impossible to reach or motivate, using old comms techniques. They are also needier.

Workers are demanding transparency, meaning, attention, and connection like never before. They want to know what you are doing beyond making a product or money.

Many expect their companies or bosses to behave like idealistic politicians, taking public stands or action on every social debate. They want evidence of heart and humanity.

Now shift from thinking about internal communications and consider how leaders and groups connect externally.

A tweet can have more influence than a national TV broadcast.

There are a dozen-plus distinct information ecosystems with distinct audiences. Think kids on TikTok, older people on Facebook, conservatives on right-wing podcasts.

A generic press release is useless in this era.

When we sit down with C-suite executives, we often find they're set up for an era that died years ago. They know it—but don't know what to do.

That poses a clear and present danger to their culture, productivity, and future success. Poor communication leads to shoddy execution, employee distrust, and most notably, the inability to get everyone on the same page.

Let this sink in: Almost every leader in every company spends most of their time communicating—yet no one teaches you how to do it efficiently, effectively, and profitably.

Here are five ways to win:

☛ **HAVE A COMMUNICATOR AT YOUR RIGHT HAND.** If you aren't a natural-born communicator with authentic expertise, your head of comms or marketing is as vital to you as your COO or your CFO.

☛ **HIRE PEOPLE FLUENT IN MODERN COMMS.** You need to know how the message you are putting forth on Twitter has to be structured differently for Facebook, for local media, for TV, and for YouTube. A few cozy relationships with reporters are useless.

☛ **RETHINK YOUR STYLE.** Chances are you talk and write too long, too fancily, too foggily. You need to be smarter, briefer, more straightforward.

☛ **BE REAL.** Most people aren't dumb. They can tell if you are being real or speaking in corporate-talking-point fakery. This is true for leaders and companywide communications. Lose the lawerly crap.

☛ **LISTEN.** It's the essential ingredient of better communications. It allows you to communicate more transparently and more authentically because you know what words, phrases, and ideas land with your audience—and which ones flop. This means more conversations with more people at more levels—your own personal focus group.

THE BOTTOM LINE. If your organization is communicating—internally or externally—with the same tone and cadence you used before this work-from-anywhere era, you're doing it wrong.

CHAPTER 38

YOU'RE A POLITICIAN

Like it or not, every leader is a politician in this era of social media pressure and workplace activism. You need to be fluent in hot cultural disputes, media savvy, and highly attuned to the competing interests of your base of employees, customers, and shareholders.

WHY IT MATTERS. Most top leaders are white, male, and over fifty, like me. Most hate the political expectations. Tough shit—it comes with the job now.

As part of a generational change that has left many corporations on the defensive, leaders are being pressured by younger workers and potential recruits—plus shareholders and customers—to take stands on issues they had always avoided addressing. This includes the divisive issues of race, guns, climate change, and LGBTQ rights.

Truth is, you don't need to take a stand on any of these topics. But you do need to be aware of the political dynamics, listen to competing viewpoints internally, and explain calmly but confidently why you are not taking a stand.

In 2019, the Business Roundtable made a small, symbolic, but significant move to push things in this direction: 181 of the nation's top CEOs agreed that driving shareholder value is no longer their sole business objective.

The CEOs expanded their mission beyond mere wealth creation to include everything from taking care of employees to helping their communities.

This shift—spearheaded by JPMorgan Chase CEO Jamie Dimon, who was then chair of the Business Roundtable—reflected the growing internal and external pressures.

Truth is, even the most press-shy, introverted leaders need to be de facto politicians. Here are some tricks for organizing your campaign:

☞ **ACCEPT THE NOMINATION.** Don't fight reality. Embrace it. People have lost trust in government, the media, and other institutions. Employers have a huge opening to fill the vacuum. The annual Edelman Trust Barometer consistently finds business is the only institution that's now perceived as being ethical and competent enough to solve the world's problems. People particularly admire their own company or companies in their own cities.

☞ **WRITE YOUR PLATFORM.** Decide what you and your company stand for and will fight for. You do not need to weigh in on all—or even any—public topic. Establish in advance what matters specifically to your organization.

☞ **CONTROL YOUR MESSAGE.** Don't wait for controversy to hit or for your opponents to define you. Talk often and openly about the issues you care about and how you choose action or silence.

☞ **DON'T LASH OUT.** Many leaders get defensive and clam up when staff demands action on a social topic. Don't. If enough people under you are worked up, gather them for a candid off-the-record discussion. Ask them to keep it in the family and respect the privacy of others. Then listen. Often people just want to be heard even if they don't get what they want.

☞ **STIR YOUR BASE.** Younger workers and applicants now insist that employers articulate their values. Previous generations were more obsessed with salaries, perks, and career paths. Stir them with your higher purpose, so they understand their work has meaning. This may make them more comfortable with your stance if you refuse the activism they demand.

THE BOTTOM LINE. Leadership is an honor, much like public service. You get to lead people through tough times and shape their minds and lives.

CHAPTER 39

TALK CRISPLY

Nothing lifted my game more than embracing a communications style we call Smart Brevity. Before it, I was a prisoner to meandering, time-sucking long-windedness just like you. Smart Brevity liberated me from the tyranny of waiting for others to make their damn point—and for me to make mine.

WHY IT MATTERS. We saw, up close, how many people and organizations were blowing the chance to be heard in this era of distraction.

So we built Axios around this idea of speaking and writing more efficiently and effectively. We built a format, tools, and eventually AI software to write our stories and communicate internally, and we run our entire company on it.

Roy, Mike, and I wrote an entire book on it: *Smart Brevity: The Art of Saying More with Less.*

If you think I'm nuts about the urgent need to change, let these stats soak in:

- The University of Maryland did extensive studies of how people read on social media, in school, and in business—and found we spend 26 seconds, on average, on things we choose to read!

· We check our phones an average of 260-plus times each day, according to a Review.org study. If you're shaking your head, I dare you to count your own glances.

· Most of what you share on social media, you didn't even read, according to our internal data at Axios. Think about that: We see a photo or headline—and get such a dopamine jolt that we just hit share like mindless lemmings.

· Gallup found that 70 percent of employees want shorter communications at work.

Despite all that, most people in schools, companies, and other organizations communicate like it's 1990—when people had more time and fewer choices.

Here are five tips to up your game:

☛ **STOP BEING SELFISH!** It is self-indulgent to force me to sort through hundreds of words to figure out what you are trying to tell me. Long-windedness and meandering are fine in some fiction and poetry. But terrible for daily life. Think about your audience, not yourself.

Pope Francis, in a 2022 speech, made a similar argument about homilies for priests. He encouraged priests worldwide to cut the length from forty to ten minutes.

It was the nuns, he said, who applauded the loudest because they are the "victims" of long homilies.

☞ **GRAB ME!** Before you write anything for Twitter, or text, or your boss or your friend group, think about the MOST important thing you want them to know. Then distill it into ONE sentence.

If you have them for only 26 seconds tops, don't hide the good stuff! Make your first sentence the most essential info, period.

☞ **WRITE AND TALK LIKE A HUMAN.** Most of us are pretty normal in conversation. But there is a defect in our species that for whatever reason when we sit down to write, we try to sound like Walt Whitman or a Harvard professor.

Authenticity and simplicity are huge winners in the era of noise.

Stop using SAT words or any word you would never use at a bar. Show-off words make people want to throw something at you, not admire you.

☞ **KEEP IT SIMPLE.** Short, tight sentences are always winners. Subject. Verb. Object.

You would never call a banana "an elongated yellow fruit" or say "prevaricate" when talking to a friend about a lie.

If you are trying to group together more than two ideas or facts, use bullet points—they are like magic for skimmers (which—face it—is everyone).

☛ **JUST STOP.** The greatest gift you can give to others and yourself is time. So use as few words and sentences and paragraphs as humanly possible. Then stop. Remember the data shows you will be lucky to get them to read 200 words, so why waste time? You can train your mind to think more crisply and deliver what matters more efficiently.

THE BOTTOM LINE. Watch how your ideas start to stick and get acted on.

PART 4

CHAPTER 40

CANDOR

"Most people think they're killing it—unless told otherwise," Mike Allen loves to remind me.

WHY IT MATTERS. People are often unaware of how they're falling short of expectations at work or in relationships—unless they're told bluntly, clearly, unambiguously.

It took me years to see this, then put it into practice myself. And it remains the hardest thing to teach most managers and employees.

Our instinct is to dance around the tough stuff—or hide it in unrelated compliments or puddles of words. We *think* we are doing this to be nice. But it's actually selfish to deny someone needed feedback.

Otherwise, the person walks away thinking . . . they're killing it.

Here's how we teach people to give the gift of candor:

☛ **BE SPECIFIC.** Leave no room for confusion. The person should know exactly what they're doing wrong or insufficiently. Don't hide it. Don't sugarcoat it.

☛ **BE TIMELY.** Most of us want to avert our gaze—it's uncomfortable to give tough feedback. But the moment you spot a pattern or problem, pounce. Every day you wait is a day the person isn't improving.

☛ **BE PRESCRIPTIVE.** Everyone deserves a chance to improve. (Most people welcome it!) Offer, with precision, what they should do differently to reverse the pattern or problem. Give a specific time frame—weeks, not months.

☛ **BE ENCOURAGING.** If they can change, tell them you believe in them and their capacity to bounce back. You just delivered sour news. Sending them into a tailspin is bad for them—and you.

☛ **BE DECISIVE.** It hurts those who are genuinely killing it if you keep problematic people around. Managers spend too much time on underperformers—a time and energy suck for the whole team.

☛ **REALITY CHECK.** This works both ways. Most managers don't seek nearly enough feedback about themselves.

As a strong, candid manager—or in a social situation, a friend—you need to give the person space to respond to your feedback.

Done right, you'll learn from each other.

THE BOTTOM LINE. Playing make-believe robs the person of the chance to step up, be better, or move on.

CHAPTER 41

JUST LISTEN

Most of us love to talk. But we suck at listening.

I'm talking about sitting quietly, with an open mind—unburdened by selfish or defensive mind spams, and soaking up what the other person is actually saying.

WHY IT MATTERS. This isn't a rant about crack-like phone addiction or gnat-sized attention spans. It's an attempt to help us—me very much included—to hear not what we *want* to hear, but what others are actually *saying*.

Imagine the relationships saved, the productivity gained, and the clarity achieved if we could better use our goofy-looking ears.

I'm blessed with a few good listeners at work, including Mike Allen and Allison Murphy, our SVP of operations. I picked their brains for some tricks for upping our listening game:

☛ **THINK FIRST.** Good listening starts before the conversation, Allison advises. Are the objectives clear? Is this about problem-solving, venting, exchanging data, brainstorming? If it's not clear, ask: "What do you need from me in this conversation?"

☞ **PUT A SOCK IN IT—CONFIDENTLY.** Think about any meeting or group dinner. Usually the person running their mouth isn't the person with the most power, the most interesting life—or the most to say. Selling something? Asking for a raise? Trying to impress a first date? You'll get to yes in the time the *other* person is talking—not when *you* are.

☞ **CLEAR THE CLUTTER.** It's impossible to listen if you're fiddling with your phone, staring at your computer, daydreaming, or simply pretending to care or listen. You need to lock in to have a fighter's chance of hearing. Your teacher was right: When you're talking, you're not learning.

☞ **STOP SELF-OBSESSING.** No one thinks you're smarter when you're babbling or filibustering or self-indulging. No one feels heard if your version of listening is silently crafting your clever comeback while they talk. This is the original sin of crappy listening. Stop committing it.

☞ **SAVOR SILENCE.** One of the oldest tricks in the book for a great interviewer is being willing to endure silence, Mike says and practices. Don't yield to our human impulse to jump in and fill the awkward pause with your random words. Let the *other person* fill the silence. What you'll learn is priceless. And you can think about what you *really* want to say, based on what they *really* said.

☛ **MONITOR FOR REPEATS.** If someone is repeating themselves, Allison explains, it is because it is (1) really important and/or (2) they don't think you're hearing them. Call it out: "You've mentioned X a few times. Can you say more?"

☛ **THEN LISTEN—TRULY AND INTENTLY.** Allison often ends a discussion or meeting by saying, "What I hear you saying is . . ." This is a masterful way to show you were listening—*and* to make sure you heard with precision what the other person was trying to convey. Don't leave space for fogginess. Force clarity—and understanding.

CHAPTER 42

READ THE ROOM

Most professionals are terrific readers. Just not of rooms.

At parties or in chats with friends, and especially in work meetings, so many are oblivious to the actual—and body—language of those around them.

WHY IT MATTERS. Imagine the tension and misunderstanding that could be averted if we were better at reading others.

The dynamics are usually obvious—if you bother to notice.

We learn to read words young—slowly and through repetition. But no one teaches you how to read others—or a room. It's more art than science and requires more EQ (emotional intelligence) than IQ.

If you can master it or even get decent at it, you'll unleash magical new powers to get more out of meetings—and those around you.

Here are a few hacks:

- **BACK TO SCHOOL.** Commit to fine-tuning your situational EQ radar. This means becoming a student of people in small group settings, be it in card games, at parties, or at work. It means wanting—and actively trying—to spot human tics, tells, and patterns. This didn't come naturally to me. It has now, through hard work and practice, grown into a vital strength.

☛ **CASE THE ROOM.** I speak to a lot of groups. It's important to know if I'm talking to farmers or pharmacists or Axios staff—and it's plain dumb and disrespectful not to find out. Know thy audience. Why are they here? Why are *you* here? Know the context of the conversation so you can spot what the room is telling you.

☛ **SHIFT YOUR EYES.** Be honest: Most of the time, you're thinking about your ideas—or dinner date—when others are talking. You're itching to read an email or check an ESPN alert. Instead, focus outward. Study what others are doing and saying. Notice body-language patterns, and what seems to motivate them or agitate them or move them.

☛ **WATCH FACES.** In a Zoom world, facial expressions are your best focal point. Same inside an actual old-fashioned room. You can tell by someone's eyes if they're paying attention. If they seem defensive, then calibrate . . . confused, clarify . . . enthused, hunt for why.

☛ **LET 'EM TALK.** If you're in a small setting and you're doing most of the talking, you're losing. Even if it's a presentation, be quick, sharp, direct—then find a way to involve others. Listen intently. Ask questions. Circle back for clarification.

☛ **DEFUSE TENSION.** Nothing good comes from escalating a situation in front of others. It rarely shows the strength you think. It often puts others on the defensive, bringing out the absolute worst in people. If you see tempers rising, the perfect escape hatch is a simple "Hey, appreciate your views. Why don't you and I chat afterward?"

☛ **TAKE NOTES.** I mean this literally and figuratively. Write down your observations and takeaways—in work meetings, in particular. It sharpens recall and keeps you focused. But also keep running notes in your head about people in the room so you can put observations into practice next time around. Mike Allen, in our exec meetings, rarely talks but always walks out with a napkin or scratch paper full of brilliant insights.

THE BOTTOM LINE. Think of the room as a book. Read the words—and between the lines.

CHAPTER 43

FILTER BS

One of the hardest things to do in leadership, and life, is to filter out BS—and filter in meaningful data and feedback—to make smart calls in chaotic moments.

The higher you rise, often the deeper the BS. People want to please you or sway you or avoid your wrath.

WHY IT MATTERS. You need a system for stress-testing your views, ideas, and self-appraisal.

Gathering the right facts or feedback boils down to genuine curiosity plus a clear-eyed analysis of experiences and people.

You're basically hunting everywhere for news, information, experiences, and voices that suggest where things are and where they're headed. Then you constantly tweak or recalibrate your views as you learn more.

Most tough things are tough precisely because there is no obvious right or wrong. There's just a bunch of opinions and options. It's your job to sift through it and make the best, right call.

Several tricks help mitigate delusion and isolation:

☛ **SMART TRUTH-TELLERS.** I'd rather hear from a wise person who knows little about me or my industry than a conventional expert. So create a web of people— usually friends or former coworkers—who seem over time to make the right decisions for the right reasons, even when it's hard. Consult them on the tough stuff.

☛ **INTIMATE TRUTH-TELLERS.** You need one or two people who know your warts and worst instincts. They tend to be so close to you that they can call out your stupidity or self-obsession. They can save you from yourself. Trust me, you'll need saving more than once.

☛ **CONFIDENT, CANDID COWORKERS.** I'm writing this book in the middle of our annual review process at Axios. I know I'll get some brutally honest feedback from my direct reports. Good. We hire smart, honest high achievers and encourage candor. It's my job to weigh the critique non-defensively and determine adjustments in style or substance.

☛ **REPORTING.** Nothing helps clarify my thinking—and enables me to gut-check my views—more than reading and talking to people across my staff and industry. Have a voracious appetite for new facts. Think of your views and analysis as living things, evolving and changing as reality shifts. Pick up the phone when someone says something that grabs you. People are willing to share more than you think.

☛ **INTELLIGENCE HACKS.** Some turn to books or raw data for critical or contrarian takes. I often turn to podcasts. You'll find experts—and your competitors—often share inside and essential information when they let their guard down on long-form podcasts. I listen to several obscure media podcasts when a CEO or head of revenue is the guest.

☛ **RELIABLE SOURCES.** You need to study your sources for accuracy over time. Be it people . . . or publications or podcasts or projections. Brian Morrissey writes a substack called The Rebooting, which goes deep into the mechanics of running media businesses. His take on the hard truth of media trends has proven very accurate, so it became a must-read for me. Roy Schwartz—our Axios cofounder, who now runs our communication software company, Axios HQ—has the best business instincts of anyone I know. So I consult him on any business move and personal investment.

☛ **FACT-PATTERN RECOGNITION.** This is the holy grail. If you have enough reliable inputs, you can start to see yourself, big decisions, and the future more clearly— and make exponentially better decisions.

THE BOTTOM LINE. You can do all of this and still get things wrong. You need to be quick to forgive yourself—but slow to simply assume it was an aberration. Study it. Learn from it. Then apply it.

CHAPTER 44

GIVING FEEDBACK

Most people hate giving—or getting—tough feedback about work, irritating behavior, or grating disagreements.

WHY IT MATTERS. Try a new approach to defuse the tension and avert snap reactions. Put it in writing first.

Truth is, most people get instantly defensive or uncomfortable if told in person, without advance notice, that they are doing something wrong or pissing you off. This makes it impossible for them to hear you fully.

Starting in the earliest days of *Politico*, cofounder John Harris and I would do this whenever there was an obvious disturbance in the force field.

Full disclosure: It didn't always erase tension. But it did allow for the issue to be articulated clearly and with ample time to digest and reflect it—before reacting and discussing it face-to-face.

This created a template I use when giving difficult feedback to a colleague or friend. Before we discuss it in person, I write them a note at least twenty-four hours in advance so they can think on it first.

Done right, writing allows you to strike a more precise and

measured tone. It lowers the emotional pitch of your voice or body language. It lets the focus be on the problem—not the instant reaction.

It also creates a written record of your efforts.

Between the lines. I stress the in-person conversation because it lets you learn something. There's always the chance you're not 100 percent right—that you have a blind spot or have missed something. So you need to listen, too.

Here's a formula that works well for me:

- ☞ **LET THEM KNOW WHAT'S COMING.** I often start such notes with "I want to share my unvarnished thoughts about X" or "You deserve to know my candid take on Y." This is a tough-love note—so don't hide it. Make clear you will follow up within a day or so with an in-person conversation.

- ☞ **THANK THEM.** Let the person know you appreciate their reading the note in the spirit in which it's intended. It's usually because you care about them personally or about their development professionally. You are writing so they can spend time reflecting on what they are about to read.

- ☞ **BE PRECISE.** This is where most people blow it. You must be unambiguous without being a total ass about the specific issue. Don't sanitize it. The recipient needs to know with total precision what must change.

☞ **DON'T PREACH.** Be clinical, not judgmental. Avoid psychoanalyzing why someone does something and focus on what needs remedying. Read it as if you were the recipient. Would a word or phrase set you off? If so, delete it.

☞ **OFFER SOLUTIONS.** Be specific about what success looks like. Tell them the behavioral change that will eliminate the issue.

☞ **BE FIRM.** Make clear the consequences if the problem persists. Maybe your relationship will worsen. Or future advancement will be impossible. Or they will be fired.

☞ **GIVE THEM HOPE.** You want to find a way to say and show there's a clear path to a remedy. Make it clear you love them or believe in them—and that if the problem is fixed, it will be forgotten.

☞ **THANK THEM AGAIN.** It's hard to get tough feedback, even if it comes from a good place. Tell the person you appreciate their reading this note and look forward to an equally direct and respectful conversation in person.

THE BOTTOM LINE. This approach sharpens your own thinking about the topic—and often illuminates nuances you miss when winging it. In the end, the process clarifies the matter for you and the recipient.

CHAPTER 45

TAKING FEEDBACK

In the summer of 2004, hours before John Kerry's nomination speech at the Democratic convention, *Washington Post* political editor Maralee Schwartz gut-punched me with some brutal feedback.

I was covering Kerry for the *Post*. I had spent that year on the road, away from my wife and kids, and this was the big front-page moment. But she said I didn't write fast enough or think big enough to capture this historic moment. John Harris (a *Post* star who later cofounded *Politico* with me) got the call instead.

I was pissed. She was right. Harris captured the speech more lyrically and insightfully than I ever could.

WHY IT MATTERS. "Feedback is a gift," the management gurus say. But in my experience running two companies, it's a gift most don't want.

It's true at work and in relationships. Every time my wife gives me feedback, I respond defensively, telling her all the reasons I rock ☺.

But learning to accept the gift with wisdom and humility is a superpower we all need. It's the gateway to growth.

Whether in a workplace or a relationship, feedback—honest, no-BS insight on what you could do better—is priceless. Too many people mess it up by talking instead of listening.

Here's my blunt feedback about taking blunt feedback:

- ☛ **LISTEN!** Don't make excuses or talk about the past. Actually, don't talk at all. Soak up, with self-confidence and humility, what the person is saying, and take time before responding. When they're finished, you can say, "Good point," if you agree . . . or "I hear you" if you want to think more about it. Or just "Thank you."

- ☛ **ASSUME POSITIVE INTENT.** The selfish approach for the other person would be to suppress what they really think. If someone has the guts to be frank with you, embrace it and thank them. When Mike asks for critiques from people, he says, "I promise to take it in the spirit it's intended."

- ☛ **DON'T BE DEFENSIVE.** That's the worst response to helpful feedback. It makes the person giving it feel unheard—and less likely to shoot straight with you in the future.

- ☛ **ASK FOR IT.** You're more likely to get feedback if you ask peers or superiors—in a sincere, humble, open-minded way—how you could be more effective. That projects strength, not weakness.

☞ **ACT ON IT.** If you show you're responsive, you'll get more input. And you'll get better at life and on the job.

☞ **CASE IN POINT.** Often when you're giving a face-to-face review, people will do the very thing you called a weakness in the written eval.

"Jim doesn't listen" or "Jim makes too many excuses" or "Jim doesn't welcome constructive criticism."

If I then tune them out, start peddling excuses, or covering my butt, I've kind of made their point.

THE BOTTOM LINE. Life is about forward motion. Elicit and take feedback to make your personal and professional performance tomorrow better than today.

CHAPTER 46

TOXIC INSECURITY

Nothing destroys more relationships, teams, or companies than insecure people in power.

WHY IT MATTERS. Beneath all bad motives, bad behavior, and bad people—at work and in life—lurks deep and dangerous insecurity.

It's an insidious form of cancer that spreads effortlessly—and quickly. Leaders who have it infect everyone and everything they touch. Leaders who tolerate this in others are complicit in crushing the souls of the inflicted. If this is you, quit leading, please.

A little insecurity is normal and healthy. So I am not talking about the natural insecure impulses that often ground us and motivate us. I am calling out the persistent and pernicious insecurity that shapes a person's character and decision-making.

So many of the lessons I have learned the hard way came from watching profoundly insecure people do the wrong thing for the wrong reason.

Two of the worst leaders I worked with at *Politico* were wholly defined by toxic insecurity. They left others feeling drained and demoralized, and often in tears. The mere mention of their names triggers scores of people who worked under them.

I wish this were a happy chapter about how not to be insecure. Take that up with your therapist—or parents. This is more about how to spot it—and crush it.

☛ **SELFISHNESS.** Anyone routinely focused on themselves—at the expense of others—has serious issues. If they do it persistently, they're unfixable. These are the people that need to loudly assert their power, or put people in their place, or speak with meanness or condescension.

☛ **SMALLNESS.** Confident people don't do petty things, like talk smack about others or stir the pot. Insecure people marinate in that crap to shift focus away from their shortcomings. If you see someone routinely doing illogical or immoral things, fire them or cut them out of your life.

☛ **BITTERNESS.** People who whine or wish ill on others are like the flu in an unventilated room. Their negativity is destined to spread and sap the energy of those around them. You can often see this in the eyes and body language of their underlings.

☛ **LONELINESS.** One telltale sign of the profoundly insecure is that they attract other insecure people—and repel confident, positive people. Don't let yourself get sucked into their misery. They often show narcissistic tendencies and seem clueless to their grossness.

☛ **MEANNESS.** Good people aren't asses. Insecure people often are. We all have bad days. But if someone seems like a bad person consistently, it's because they are one.

THE BOTTOM LINE. I wasted years of my life believing I could change insecure leaders. You can't. I will never fully forgive myself for allowing the jerks to ruin others. Don't repeat my mistake.

CHAPTER 47

TOXIC AMBIGUITY

One of the most overlooked yet lethal forms of organizational cancer is toxic ambiguity. Basically, killing people with fog.

WHY IT MATTERS. Think of all the time wasted, relationships ruined, budgets missed, and moods fouled by leaders offering hazy direction. Most notes from most CEOs—especially publicly traded ones—read like they were written with the ChatGPT prompt *Write something no human could finish or understand.* A great deal of the feedback from most managers reads like they typed in the prompt *Write something so banal it camouflages your actual views.*

Ambiguity is a silent killer, like a slow natural gas leak. You don't realize until it's too late you have a massive, spreading issue.

Gallup developed a workplace survey system for companies to track engagement and performance. We use it at Axios to spot pockets of emerging staff issues. We often score lower than I'd like on whether "I know what is expected of me at work." This drives me nuts: How can any person at any level not know what their damn job is?

Turns out, this is common. Most people feel foggy even if leaders feel they are being crystal clear.

The toxicity comes when the ambiguity is so thick others can exploit—or suffer from—the cloudiness. Here are some common manifestations to watch for:

- ☛ **FUZZY STRATEGY.** In an ideal world, any person working under you should be able to jump out of bed at a moment's notice and recite the three most important things you're doing as a company. If they can't, how can they guide others or prioritize? The only remedy for this is constant clear repetition of what matters most.

- ☛ **FUZZY THINKING.** If you cannot articulate those three things with precision and certainty, you're screwed. It means you didn't sharpen your own thinking before sharpening the thinking of others. This is why I constantly write down what matters most so I can stress-test my own clarity.

- ☛ **FUZZY COMMUNICATIONS.** You might have strong, concrete thoughts but explain them mushily. That's akin to having the perfect recipe for something delicious but not cooking it for anyone. And then wondering why people don't love your dish. Your ideas might be brilliant, but if you don't find strong, memorable words to express them, they will be lost.

☛ **FUZZY ACCOUNTABILITY.** This one often trips me up. People do not know they own something unless they are explicitly told and empowered. And others do not know who to listen to unless you make it clear who's the decider. Little gets done right without clear accountability dictated and announced in advance.

☛ **FUZZY FEEDBACK.** Few things cripple individuals, teams, and companies more than foggy feedback. Most are scared to be direct and hide what they mean by overtalking and overcomplimenting. This leaves people confused about their standing and what they need to do better. Confused people are more prone to insecurity and bad behaviors. Do them a favor: be unambiguous.

CHAPTER 48

BAD BOSSES

It's hard enough to give candid feedback to a friend or subordinate. Giving it to your *boss* is one of the most difficult things to do—and can get you booted if you botch it.

WHY IT MATTERS. Very few of us make it through life without running into a moronic, mushy, or mediocre manager. But there are ways to raise concerns directly, safely, and effectively.

I botched my first stab at it, quite spectacularly. I was at *Roll Call,* in the mid-1990s, when a fellow journalist, Ed Henry, was put in charge of the newsroom. A few of us thought he was wrong for the job, so I impulsively went to the bosses, winged it with no forethought, made it way too personal, pitched myself as an alternative, and . . . lost. Ed's boss listened politely . . . and then sided with Ed. He remained editor.

I did everything the Jim of today would counsel young Jim not to do. Now, thirty years later, having watched others do this well and poorly, I see a clear blueprint:

- ☞ **SHARPEN YOUR THINKING.** What exactly is the boss doing that's making it harder for you or others to thrive?

☛ **DO A GUT CHECK.** Discuss your issue with a friend, family member, or mentor—ideally someone not involved at your company. Lay out your concerns without hyperbole, then lay out dispassionately the defense your manager might make.

☛ **WRITE IT DOWN.** I am a big believer that you can be more precise and measured if you put your concerns in writing. Be respectful. Be direct. Say you appreciate the chance to share your unvarnished thoughts.

☛ **EXPLAIN, DON'T ACCUSE.** You put someone instantly on the defensive if you hammer them or question their character. Be very specific, clinical, and unemotional in how you frame your concerns.

☛ **OFFER SOLUTIONS.** No one wants to hear someone simply bitch about problems or grievances. Offer specific solutions or alternative approaches.

☛ **LOCK ARMS.** Make it plain that you want to be part of the solution. People who feel isolated, backed into corners, or judged typically retaliate or hide.

☛ **FOLLOW UP.** Ask for a follow-up conversation, in person, after they have digested your note, to discuss the next steps. How they respond will give you a very strong indication of whether the situation is fixable.

☞ **GIVE 'EM A CHANCE.** Change is hard. Watch to see if a correction is made. If not, politely but directly remind them of your note and chat.

💣 **TRUTH BOMB.** Just because someone gets power does not mean they deserve it. A lot of bad or talentless people rise to management by bootlicking or tenure.

☞ **CONFRONT REALITY.** Most middle managers, in my experience, are hard to change. If someone does not listen to you respectfully or refuses to change, be ready to live with the status quo . . . or quit.

THE BOTTOM LINE. Great bosses are like firm—but unconditionally loving—parents. Embrace them. Bad ones are like duplicitous ex-boyfriends or -girlfriends who suck the life out of you. Try to fix it. But if nothing changes, run if you can.

CHAPTER 49

GOOD BOSSES

We've all had (or have!) crappy bosses—the arrogant, self-obsessed, know-it-all frauds who soil our work lives. That's why the good ones are worth studying and treasuring.

WHY IT MATTERS. Hunt for an unusual combination of smarts, emotional intelligence, toughness, and humility. Then you know you've truly unearthed one.

If you do find one, treasure them—and study the hell out of them. These skills are learnable and contagious . . . and applicable to every part of your life.

I'm not talking about great bosses as measured by financial performance or public image. Those are often mirages. We too often celebrate astonishing feats done by astonishing asses.

I'm talking about bosses who leave you not just better at your job, but a better person overall. This, to me, is the holy grail of managerial exceptionalism.

I'm talking here about managers or bosses, not necessarily leaders—the women and men with direct reports who offer daily guidance to individuals and give regular direction, correction, and compliments.

● **TRUTH BOMB:** Middle management bosses are often the

weakest part of a company, smooshed between high-achieving executives above and ambitious individual contributors below.

They're often promoted because they did well in their individual role. The logical next step led to middle management. Too often, companies suck at training these people to be excellent managers of other people.

Some telltale signs of great managers:

- ☛ **SMARTS.** This is usually a mix of subject expertise and street smarts. It's hard to be a mediocre mind or talent and a great manager.

- ☛ **HUMILITY.** The job, by definition, is to serve others. Good managers care more about the performance of others than about their own egos.

- ☛ **COOL HEAD.** People are weird. They do unpredictable things for mystifying reasons. Strong managers don't allow temper or emotion to boil over.

- ☛ **TOUGH MIND.** The best bosses are direct, clear, and firm. They don't dance around tough feedback or duck tough decisions. They demand respect, not love.

- ☛ **TONE-SETTING.** They lead by example, never asking others for anything they don't deliver (or overdeliver) themselves. This spans work ethic, values, and performance.

☛ **HUNGRY.** They're never fully satisfied—always pushing for you, the team, and the company to be better tomorrow than today. A complacent manager dulls ambition.

☛ **INVOLVED.** They're students of their staff. They teach, inspire, and provide regular feedback and advice. It's not enough to simply lead by example. Most of us need more than that.

CHAPTER 50

HEALTHY REVENGE

In the summer of 2021, Mathias Döpfner, the billionaire CEO of Axel Springer, a German media conglomerate, asked for an urgent meeting. He wanted to send a private plane to Appleton, Wisconsin, where nearby I was attending my aunt's funeral, to fly me to Sun Valley. It was time sensitive—and confidential, he insisted.

At a small café on the outskirts of an annual gathering for media moguls, Döpfner and Henry Kravis, the cofounder of KKR, one of the largest private equity firms in the world, dropped a big surprise on my lap. They wanted to buy Axios and *Politico*—and put me in charge of both. It was a chance to keep my new baby, Axios, and get my old one, *Politico*, back. They warned I would need to keep it top secret, knowing Robert Allbritton would never sell *Politico* if he knew I was taking it over. Oh, this felt like sweet revenge—for about one second. Then I realized I had no interest in the concept—or scheme. I was loving life at Axios, and the thought of fixing a publication I left years ago sounded like a drag.

We kept talking. Axel was proposing to buy us for north of

$400 million, so it was hard to simply walk away. But the more we talked, the shadier Döpfner's double-dealing and secret-keeping felt. So we took a pass on a life-changing outcome.

Döpfner ended up buying *Politico* for $1 billion instead. My lust for revenge was strong. I wanted payback for wasting months of my life.

WHY IT MATTERS. Even at fifty-two—despite knowing in calm times that it's wasted energy—when wronged, I want to fight. I want revenge. This remains one of my most difficult emotions to tame.

The lust for vengeance lurks in all of us. But acting on it almost never satisfies us. In fact, it often makes us feel worse.

Psychological and behavioral scientists found the mere thought of revenge stimulates the part of our brain that processes reward. Yet the reward is rarely realized:

- Instead of making us feel better, revenge prolongs our bitterness; we continue to feel wronged. When we obsess about the slight, it keeps tormenting us.

- Instead of delivering the justice you think you deserve (and might deserve!), revenge often creates a cycle that drags things out even longer.

- Plus you often feel like a jerk—when you were the victim.

So how do we tame an impulse as old as our species?

☞ **GET AN ANTI-VENGEANCE COUNSELOR.** This should
be a smart, trusted friend or mentor who can listen to
you vent, then steer you toward a sane response.

☞ **SIT ON YOUR RAGE.** Never retaliate immediately. The
worst thing you can do is respond impulsively.

The only thing worse than revenge is . . . regrettable
revenge. Anything you want to write or say, sleep on it
for a few days before acting. Most of the time, you'll
come to your senses.

☞ **BRUSH IT OFF.** It's different if the person has hurt your
character or family. But most of the time, whatever
you're stewing about isn't that big a deal in the scheme
of things, anyway.

Is this something that'll matter in ten years? If not,
move on!

☞ **DON'T BOTTLE IT UP.** I find it therapeutic to write—but
not send—a retaliatory email. Or I simply share my fury
with a friend.

This lets you release the steam in a healthier fashion.
If you just let it build silently and alone, you're more
likely to explode.

☞ **VENGEANCE IN MODERATION.** This is a tricky one—
but it works. Letting revenge animate your decision is

obviously stupid, and usually wrong. But allowing yourself a sip or two of thinking about vengeance can be invigorating.

It motivates us to prove that person and others wrong.

THE BOTTOM LINE. Use the negative energy for a positive outcome—upping your game to be better than the jerk who wronged you.

Mere months after the collapse of the Axel deal, Alex Taylor, the CEO of Cox Enterprises, called and asked about buying Axios for all the right reasons. He believed in clinical nonpartisan journalism, admired our culture, and appreciated how we conducted business. In September of 2022, Taylor bought a majority stake in Axios at a valuation of $525 million.

Now that's sweet—and healthy—revenge.

CHAPTER 51

UNWINNABLE WARS

Roger Ailes—then the godfather of Fox News and one of the most powerful people in media—hated *Politico* from the get-go.

Ailes, who died in 2017, blacklisted *Politico* journalists from Fox News after Fred Ryan, our publisher, leveraged his role as head of the Ronald Reagan Presidential Library to land two presidential debates for *Politico*.

The library picked CNN and MSNBC as partners over Fox. Ailes was livid.

Plus Ben Smith, then a *Politico* blogger, wrote a story Ailes hated. So Fox News would routinely (and inaccurately) refer to *Politico* as "left-wing."

WHY IT MATTERS. When we launched *Politico*, we recognized Ailes's deliberate effort to stoke an us-vs.-everyone culture to do the impossible—create a new dominant cable-news empire.

In the end, Ailes taught me: Some wars are unwinnable. Some people are unchangeable.

The blacklisting hurt us. We were a new publication hell-bent on appealing to conservatives and liberals alike. Fox was, and remains, dominant in its space.

We had countless meetings and episodic back-channeling—even a lunch in the Fox executive dining room—to try to defuse things. Nothing worked. In 2013, Ailes wanted to talk and was furious again.

Peace offerings weren't working. I decided that aggressors respond only to blunt force. So I let it fly.

Knowing this would be a hoot, two colleagues—Danielle Jones and Kim Kingsley—popped into my office to witness the showdown.

When Ailes came on the line, he was fuming about Dylan Byers's write-up of a book about President Obama by Jonathan Alter that portrayed Ailes as paranoid.

Ailes yelled at me about Alter "writing in his underwear," and how he would "not take any shit from Dylan Byers," based on detailed notes I took for a diary of my time at *Politico*.

Ailes screamed: "I did not think he was an intellectual, because that's what all you left-wing nuts think."

My response, again thinking blunt force might work: "Roger, go f— yourself."

Roger: "Wait! What? You just told Roger Ailes to go f—himself.

"Stick it in your damn ear!" he shouted. "You just said that so you could tell people you told Roger Ailes to go f— himself."

No, I replied. I wanted him to stop calling us liberal.

Ailes got creepy, warning of a coming war against us. Dylan, he warned, "will either fall off the limb or have the limb sawed off." I said that was a threat. He said it was not.

He screamed something about my thinking he was a wimp and dared us to come to Fox and call him a wimp. He hung up.

For twenty-four hours, I thought I was right. A top Ailes adviser called and suggested a truce would be possible now—maybe via an in-person lunch.

Then . . . crickets. We never talked again and remained blacklisted until Ailes was forced out of Fox years later.

THE BOTTOM LINE. Some fights simply can't be won—but make for fun stories to end a section of a book.

All of us flirt with unwinnable fights with unsavory characters. The trick is knowing which ones are worth picking. There's liberation in knowing some wars are unwinnable and some people are unchangeable.

PART 5

CHAPTER 52

LITTLE THINGS

My eighty-year-old dad, John VandeHei, pulled me aside during a recent pilgrimage to my homeland—Oshkosh, Wisconsin—with a deep thought on life.

Reflecting on the stuff that sticks eight decades into life, he handed me a note from his granddaughter (my oldest niece), Ally, and said, "It's the little things." They are the big things.

Ally's note wasn't about an exotic trip or some fancy gift or gesture. It was about burnt-out bulbs on an old string of Christmas lights.

Turns out, for fourteen years, Ally and my dad would tend to the lights on the trees outside their house. It's one of the small traditions no one else would notice. But this year, for the first time, one string was dead.

Here are Ally's words in a holiday note to my dad:

The one strand of lights that burned out sat in my hands as I was about to throw them away. I took a step back and reflected on the joy that this single strand of $5 lights gave to us in the past 13 years. I immediately rummaged through your tool cabinets to find scissors of some sort. I cut apart a handful of the bulbs before throwing it away.

I wanted to make sure you had a bulb. I have one myself. It's our little thing, Papa. It is a reminder of the celebration of us. These bulbs have watched our lives fly by.

My dad's broken bulb dangles on the lamp next to his favorite chair. Her note sits folded on the table beside him.

WHY IT MATTERS. Well, when your dad drops some wisdom and tells you to write it down, ya do it.

His observation really hit home for me as I reflected on my son James, my mini-me, heading off to college. The good stuff is the small stuff: the long talks, Katahdin hikes, inside jokes, COVID workouts, Packer Sundays, little rituals. That's the stuff you miss as the clock ticks.

This sounds so simple and cliche. But it's kinda the secret of a life well lived. Yes, do big things and grand acts. Win awards. Make money. Travel the world. But it's all meaningless unless you savor little joys with people you love.

Here are a few ways to think about the little things:

- ☛ **CREATE LITTLE THINGS.** It's so easy to get lost in big gifts or grand adventures. In a world moving so fast, brimming with so many distractions, take time for small acts or small rituals. I see how much my macho son longs for those soft moments despite his grunts. He wandered around the house those final days before college basically begging for attention and small moments.

☛ **WRITE IT DOWN**. Memories fade. Keep notes of those little moments that pop. We all need a diary, whether it's pecked on your phone or written old-school on actual paper. Watch for patterns. Soak up the wisdom packed inside. And then . . .

☛ **EXPRESS IT.** Of all the cool things I experienced at the *Washington Post* in the mid-2000s, including covering the presidency, one thing stuck most: a few very short handwritten notes from publisher Don Graham applauding a story I had written. I tucked each one into a drawer and savored them. I'm sure thousands of others did, too. Never underestimate the power of a few thankful words.

☛ **SAVOR IT.** It's easy to doom-scroll yourself through social media into depression or hopelessness. Reminding yourself of the thousands of small acts of kindness and meaning in the real world is the perfect antidote.

CHAPTER 53

WHAT MATTERS

I'll never forget asking Mike Allen, my cofounder at Axios and *Politico* and one of America's most famous journalists, how he grew kinder as his public prominence—and power—soared.

"I don't understand how you could not get humbler. It's obvious how much luck and help it took to get me here," he said.

WHY IT MATTERS. We often celebrate those who break things, invent things, or build things with bravado. But I have learned more studying two men of uncommon modesty: Mikey and the late Fred Rogers, aka Mister Rogers.

They both put a lot of deep thought and work not into *what* they wanted to be but *who*. And studying their character is a good way to shape your own.

Mike is a journalistic superstar, featured on the cover of the *New York Times Magazine* as "The Man the White House Wakes Up To."

We've been close friends, fellow journalists, and/or business partners since we met on the deck of a cruise ship more than two decades ago. I was a reporter for the *Wall Street Journal*, he for the *Washington Post*. We both covered the White House.

Trade protests were ravaging the port city of Genoa, Italy. So they parked a cruise ship to house the journalists there to cover President George W. Bush. It was four a.m., and I walked up to the bar. Mike elbowed me, bought me a beer, and challenged me to a slamming contest. He won. But I won a lifelong muse.

Fred Rogers was a true American legend. *Mister Rogers' Neighborhood* spanned a thousand episodes—at the time, the longest-running and most popular children's program. He was a cultural icon and a fierce defender of kids and critic of television, and he did this longer than anyone else on television.

The two are similar in subtlety and selflessness. Their common gifts do not come easily to most, me included:

☞ **AUTHENTIC HUMILITY.** Both have a total absence of "Look at me!" spotlight-seeking you often see in others. They position themselves as servants or beneficiaries, not superiors. They both make others feel in conversation like the most important person in the world.

☞ **INTENSE INTEREST IN OTHERS.** Both ask so many questions it initially seems like deflection, even insincerity. They're maddeningly private. But then you realize their superpower is wild curiosity about what really makes others tick. Think of all you learn when you're intensely listening.

☞ **UNUSUAL OPTIMISM.** I am a skeptic by training, a realist by default. Mike always sees the goodness in people and situations. I am way more of a realist (brutally so), while Mike is a total optimist. His glass is not just half full but spilling over with the Best Water Ever. Fred Rogers was the same, speaking to the child inside all of us.

☛ **MINIMALIST LIVING.** No fancy mansions. No splashy sports cars. Hell, Mike doesn't even have his own car or cable service. He spends more on donuts for Axios colleagues than he does on clothes.

☛ **DEEP FAITH.** Most of the impressive people I meet in life hold a deep belief in something beyond themselves. And it shows without saying. It typically manifests itself in grace and generosity with others. But it also shines in their quiet confidence and wise, selfless decision-making in difficult moments.

THE BOTTOM LINE. Fred Rogers had this wonderful ritual he would encourage others to do. Close your eyes for one minute and picture all the people who helped you get where you are today.

CHAPTER 54

THE NEXT RIGHT THING

In 2016, I sat in a pew at church, stewing about a work aggravation. David Glade, the preacher, seemed to know how to help. He started talking about the difficulties of being good.

He told a story about how his kids wondered how—with all the chaos and challenges of life—a person can choose to do the right thing, always.

Reverend Glade offered nine words of wisdom that guided me through that problem—and shape how I try to live today: "All you can do is the next right thing."

WHY IT MATTERS. What might have been a throwaway phrase in a random sermon has served as a mantra for how I run my company and my life. It helps settle me when I hit turbulence inside or outside work.

Regardless of your stage of life, you may find it hard to blow off slights, make good choices, live an upstanding life.

A small group of us built *Politico*. I came up with the idea, my wife named it, and Mike and a small group of us willed it into existence. Ten years later, Robert Allbritton, who funded the company, was trying to screw us out of millions of dollars and playing scummy legal maneuvers. So we were quitting to start Axios.

I wanted to fight, go public with the real story, and retaliate. Doing the right thing felt impossible. But this mantra saved me from my worst impulses. My instinct is to fight NOW and show the other person how right or righteous I am. In this specific instance, I wanted to go public with the ugly details of what I saw as detestable small-minded behavior. But that would only hurt people I cared about and prolong what was already an extended dispute.

The simplicity of just getting the next thing right helped immeasurably.

- ☞ **IT'S DOABLE.** It's overwhelming, with everything that hits us in life, to deal with the enormity of always doing the right thing. But if you just think about the right thing in the single moment staring at you at that moment, it usually becomes easy.

- ☞ **IT'S CLARIFYING.** We do have a choice in every tough situation, even when we feel wronged. Taking a deep breath and asking yourself what's the right response will put everything in proper perspective.

- ☞ **IT'S LIFE-ENHANCING.** So much in life is habit. You can create a healthy habit of making good decisions if you stack small hard but good decisions on top of one another. Think of it in terms of a fight-or-fight impulse. There is no flight in me. So I need to start small by never responding to any slight in the moment. Then I have to write down my reaction and sit on it for a while. Next I consult with people I trust who know me—Mike or my dad or my wife or kids. Then over time I see how often the right response is no response and usually (but not always) just move on instantly without having to go through all those small steps. These small habits, once stacked, became a way of life.

☞ **START SMALL.** If you think about big career or relationship decisions, it's easy to get paralyzed by trying to apply game theory to your next big gig or marriage. It's much easier to fixate on getting the immediate move correct.

THE BOTTOM LINE. It's shocking how often at work—and in life—people around us seem to do the wrong thing for the wrong reason. The truth is, it's often easier to stay silent when a boss mistreats people or to join in griping about a difficult coworker. It takes effort, and often some modicum of courage, to do what deep down you know is right. Usually, our sin is laziness or ambivalence—thinking we did not do anything especially wrong. But doing nothing is doing the wrong thing for the wrong reason (too much work to do the right thing). The antidote to this is actively thinking through the right response—what would you want your kids or your parents to SEE you do?—and then doing it.

CHAPTER 55

DON'T FLINCH

Well into my late twenties, I often flinched at giving money to a homeless person, rationalizing that I might be enabling laziness or drug use. Washington's streets are full of people begging for money, so it made my life easier to simply ignore them.

Autumn, my wife, is the opposite. She always gives money and engages every person in need. She was a social worker helping abused kids before spending more than a decade spotlighting—and then working for legislation against—domestic sex trafficking of kids in America.

One day, with our two young kids in the backseat, she pushed back against my view after handing twenty dollars to a homeless man, saying, "If I'm going to make a mistake, I want to err on the side of giving a drug addict money rather than not giving a hungry person means to eat that day."

She changed my mind about generosity. More important, she inspired our kids (on their good days) to adopt a similar "help, don't hide" approach to people in need.

WHY IT MATTERS. We all have chances to help those struggling instead of looking the other way—or justifying doing nothing. This mindset applies to friendship, work, leadership, and life. Pay close attention to others, and when people hit rough spots, take notice—and help.

What this might look like in regular life or at work:

- ☛ **IF YOU SEE NEED, ACT.** It is so easy to see someone in need, on the street or in the office, and convince yourself it's none of your business—or that someone else will step up. It's uncomfortable to speak up or step up when others don't respond. Be the one who takes action.

- ☛ **IF YOU WONDER, ASK.** I am an introvert, so my natural instinct is to keep to myself. People like me need to force themselves to simply ask if someone needs a hand when things seem off. This remains a struggle for me. But I never regret pushing outside my comfort zone.

- ☛ **ERR ON THE SIDE OF GENEROSITY.** Autumn is right. Are you ever going to feel bad about giving money or time to others? Never. "Our job is to give. Let God decide if the recipient did good with your gift," she says.

- ☛ **SURROUND YOURSELF WITH GIVERS.** All habits are contagious. Between Autumn and my parents, who give all their time and focus to their kids even though we're adults, I am surrounded by givers. It can't help but rub off.

☞ **OTHERS ARE WATCHING.** You will be surprised how many watch and copy you. All actions are contagious— and goodness spreads just as easily as badness.

☞ **ZOOM IN.** At Axios, chief of staff Kayla Cook Brown, our first hire before we had a name or an office, is the heart and soul of our company. She's our don't-look- away specialist, always aware of who's up, who's down. She'll constantly point out who needs a pick-me-up— and usually know the perfect word or gesture for the moment.

THE BOTTOM LINE. Every person and workplace need Kaylas.

CHAPTER 56

STREET SMARTS

I have spent years trying to teach my kids that true wisdom and smarts come in many forms.

One form is two barrel-bellied, cheap-beer-swilling, gray-bearded, f-word hurling, meat-eating, bighearted, proud rural Mainers. They died within three days of each other in 2022.

WHY IT MATTERS. Jeff and David Worcester, the Worcester brothers, taught me—and my kids, family, and friends—about old cars and exotic motors, Maine lore, remote fishing lakes, and hidden four-wheel trails to nowhere.

They were gentle giants—and geniuses, in their unique ways. You will run across many Worcester brothers in your life, people who might not look like role models or wisewomen or sages. Don't let appearance or job titles or money fool you— some of the smartest people come in surprising shapes and sizes. Listen. Learn.

Jeff and David were my wife's cousins. But over the last two decades, they became my family, too. I would just sit and soak up their earthy smarts over beers in what David proudly called "Asshole's Garage," or on Jeff's fishing boat in remote ponds.

Both died too young, in their sixties. Maine lost a big chunk of its soul.

The burly Worcester brothers left behind some awesome wisdom and values I hope live on with my kids—and resonate with you.

- ☞ **CAMOUFLAGED SMARTS.** David was a redneck fashionista—the cruder and more obnoxious the T-shirt, the better. Think f-words and middle fingers. Get him talking about rare cars, broken motors, or physics, and he was off-the-charts smart—an unalloyed nerd.

  Jeff had a de facto master's degree in Maine, an encyclopedic knowledge of every lake, every animal and fish species, every hidden trail through forgotten forests. He was a four-season outdoor wonder. It was mesmerizing.

- ☞ **NO BS.** They were never condescending. I am a dope when it comes to mechanics and was new to Maine's countless lakes, filled with landlocked salmon, togue, and splake.

  They patiently shared their knowledge and never made anyone feel stupid or small for naiveté.

- ☞ **NO PRETENSE.** David smoked like a chimney and drank Natural Light like water. Jeff scuffed at anything that didn't say Milwaukee's Best, maybe the worst-tasting beer known to man. Their diet seemed to consist of miscellaneous meats. But they were content.

☞ **GENEROSITY.** Nothing brought me more joy than bringing family and friends to Maine to fish with Jeff. He would pack the food, grab the bait, and spend hours with any city slicker wanting to wet a line.

I can think of a dozen friends who speak of him like a mythical Sherpa, a fishing and trail guide from the heavens. He opened their eyes to the outdoor magic of Maine. He is a big reason for my Maine obsession.

At every family gathering, they worked the grill, pulled the tubers, played with the kids. David would steal away the kids to let them ride in—or illegally drive—his latest antique car.

☞ **SHOW UP.** That's not a bad legacy for any of us—taking enough interest in enough people to be unforgettable and irreplaceable. They showed up, they shared, and they cared. They left a big damn mark.

THE BOTTOM LINE. There is so much wisdom outside the big cities, the college campuses, and the white-collar workforce—seek it and soak it up. It's precious stuff, folks. RIP, Worcester brothers.

CHAPTER 57

IMPROVISE

My daughter Sophie's high school art teacher, Kate Elkins, told her to never throw away a canvas. Finish the piece, even if you hate it. Improvise.

WHY IT MATTERS. This was brought home to Sophie even more powerfully when she met a Ukrainian artist, Anatolii Tarasiuk, who showed Sophie, and all of us, just how far you can stretch that canvas.

Sophie is a senior at the University of North Carolina, Chapel Hill, minoring in journalism. When she was a junior, she picked the art scene to cover for her semester-long reporting class.

This brought her to Anatolii, a Ukrainian artist currently living just outside of Chapel Hill. A year ago, he was trapped with his family in Kiev, Ukraine, when Russia invaded.

"In the morning when all the sirens started to sound simultaneously, it was so surreal to look outside to see how people were trying to leave the city," he told Sophie. "But the road was blocked. Nobody was going anywhere."

He wanted to flee. But a new wartime law prevented it: No men were allowed to depart unless they were sixty or older, handicapped, or had three children younger than eighteen. At the time, Anatolii had two young sons and his wife was pregnant.

So he improvised—and waited.

A few months into the war, their third baby boy was born. "We could actually hear rockets flying above the houses where we were staying," he recalled. Now they could flee.

Anatolii refused to leave without his art. He traveled back to Kiev to grab forty-five of his pieces to bring to America. But a nagging health issue demanded a look.

So he improvised—and prayed.

Anatolii traveled to a medical center in Kremenchuk, Ukraine. After he saw the doctor, his wife wanted to hit the local mall, despite the danger.

He improvised—for her—and said no. He was too tired.

While they were on their way out of Kremenchuk, smoke choked the distant sky. The shopping mall, located on the same street he'd just left, had been bombed.

In Poland, his phone rang. It was the medical center he had visited on his way out of town. He had cancer, the doctor told him.

So he improvised—and flew to America with no job, no insurance. Just cancer.

Anatolii wound up in Durham, North Carolina. Little did he know he was near the Duke Cancer Institute—the best medical facility for his type of cancer. He met a friend who helped him get first-class treatment.

The treatment worked. As of December 2022, he was cancer-free.

So he improvised—back into art.

By pure chance, Anatolii heard of the Artist Frame Hub, a program by the the Frame & Print Shop in Chapel Hill, North Carolina, providing framing for local artists.

So he took a few of his forty-five pieces of art, rolled tight to survive his transatlantic journey, and showed them to Becky Woodruff, the co-owner. She was inspired by his wild story.

So she improvised—and hosted an exhibition spotlighting fifteen of his best works. It was called "New Beginnings."

Anatolii was soon awarded a studio—free—at nearby Eno Arts Mill.

And he was back to improvising with his brush.

"When I start, I have an idea or image in mind of what I'm about to do," he said. "I don't have any print drawings. I just start with a palette of what I think is good for today."

He improvises from there. "It's kind of having a little expectation everywhere, in every way. In life and in art."

Recently, Anatolii learned his cancer had returned. "I'm going to keep fighting," he said.

Anatolii headed to his studio and once more turned to his art. He mixed up too much oil paint and ended up staying late into the night to use it all.

He improvised . . . creating three new pieces.

Anatolii's dramatic story reminded me how much a start-up, daily business decisions, relationships, and life is about improvising in scary or uncertain moments that help define us. You too can take these lessons with you:

☛ **IMPROVISATION WILL BE AN ESSENTIAL SKILL** and mentality in a world shaped by artificial intelligence.

☛ **THE VELOCITY OF CHANGE** in coming years will be neck-snapping. It demands the on-the-fly agility modeled by Anatolii.

CHAPTER 58

SERVE OTHERS

The best people and leaders put their friends, colleagues, and company above their own ambition. They serve others—or the cause—and it makes others, consciously or subconsciously, want to please or serve them. They basically secure more power or authority by focusing on others first.

WHY IT MATTERS. This probably sounds impossible or absurd. But it works wonders, from entry level to CEO. The sooner you put it into practice, the more you will succeed. Really.

It's often the wild CEOs with cutthroat attitudes who get featured in books or in HBO shows. But the most successful—and happy—people realize their own selfish ambitions by genuinely serving others.

Think of all the benefits:

☛ **PEOPLE CHEER FOR YOU.** Particularly in this era of valuing inclusion and purpose at work, people want to do things for people who do things for others. This is like a magnet, attracting other talented people of quality character who want and cheer for you to succeed. You in turn benefit.

☞ **PEOPLE DON'T ROOT AGAINST YOU.** You can win a battle or an early promotion by being an ass or hiding your self-obsession. But it will bite you or bring you down eventually because others plot or cheer for your fall. At the very least, if you are in for just you, all you will find is a lonely win. Both outcomes blow.

☞ **YOU WILL THRIVE.** There is a massive surge in companies seeking leaders with soft skills, including high emotional intelligence. The next wave of great leaders will have a healthy mix of strong opinions and intuition, risk-taking courage, and high EQ. They will be and be seen as smart, high-achieving servants.

☞ **YOU WILL BE A BETTER PERSON.** We're all selfish and ambitious in some respects. That's actually great: such qualities can motivate and stimulate you. But if you can train yourself to be more selfless—by freezing big moments in your mind and looking at them through others' eyes—you'll see big returns.

THE BOTTOM LINE. This works in business and life. Mike Allen is the one who turned me on to the power of it at work.

He noted how he always treats everyone the same, regardless of status, and always looks for chances to serve. The baggage boy he treats kindly on presidential trips might one day be a chief of staff—and an amazing source.

He doesn't do this because he wants something in return. But he's amazed at how often those same people do big things for him down the road.

Here's the best part: You can train yourself to do this.

- Start small. Look for one chance each week to help a colleague, your team, or a friend—and seek no credit for it.

- Check back six months later. I bet you'll see a noticeable improvement in your relationships, standing, and happiness.

CHAPTER 59

POSITIVE INTENT

We're all paranoid. We assume someone was lying or manipulative or some kind of plotting dope when we're wronged, especially at work, especially when we hardly know the person.

It happens all the time at Axios. Someone comes to me with a gripe about getting cut out of a meeting or disrespected by a peer. Nine times out of ten, they're flat wrong. The other person simply forgot to hit send on email or was struggling with personal crap at home.

WHY IT MATTERS. So much misunderstanding, tension, and turmoil flow from thinking the other person is out to get you. So stop assuming the worse. Assume positive intent instead.

It's shocking how often the explanation is so much simpler and more benign. And how often the simple question—is that what you intended?—would clarify things.

Dig deep enough into rotten relationships or business cultures, and you often find bad assumptions in the roots. Telltale signs are suspicion, backbiting, or score-settling.

Yes, some people actually are rotten . . . or dishonest . . . or truly out to get you. You shouldn't ignore patterns of toxic behavior. But most people are simply stressed . . . or clumsy with their words . . . or innocently screwing up.

Here are a few ways to think about shifting to an assumption of positive intent:

- ☞ **ASK.** You never know what's going on in someone's life. Maybe they just got a horrible medical diagnosis, or had an awful bill come due, or had a relationship fall apart. If someone seems off or down, ask. Most of life's problems can be solved instantly if you calmly and clearly ask someone who offended or irritated you what they intended to do or say. Don't ask in a condescending or aggressive way.

  Then listen.

  Do this one thing in person and you'll ease lots of tension.

- ☞ **TALK, DON'T TEXT.** Typing words is a terrible way to capture the nuance of human emotion. You cannot resolve tension at work or in your personal life on Twitter or in texts. Pick up the phone or go old-school and actually talk to a person *in person*.

- ☞ **DON'T TALK CRAP.** At Axios, we make it super-clear that we're intolerant of anyone talking about colleagues behind their backs. It's a fireable offense. You're expected to take your grievances directly to the person, honestly and respectfully.

  The only thing worse than assuming negative intent

is gossiping about it and spreading the problem. That's how Small Things Become Big Things.

☛ **DON'T WAIT.** If you feel wronged, don't marinate in the fury. Confront it calmly but immediately. And if your bruised feelings were misplaced, don't wait to move on. Life is too short to be spooked by ghosts.

CHAPTER 60

QUIET GREATNESS

David Rogers—a gruff, exacting, idiosyncratic former congressional reporter for the *Wall Street Journal*—is the best journalist I've come across.

David, now retired, was my mentor—and sometimes tormentor—in the 2000s, when I was a rising congressional and White House reporter.

WHY IT MATTERS. David taught me a master class, by actions more than words, about what it takes to be the very best at your craft.

Not good. Not content. But better than anyone else who does what you do. To me, this is what every person should aspire to. Why settle for fine? There's no market for mediocrity.

FIRST, THE BACKSTORY. To this day, I'm convinced I got my big break in journalism because of David, unwittingly so. I was a congressional reporter in my late twenties, and the *Journal* rarely hired young reporters for their Capitol Hill gigs back then.

But Alan Murray, the Washington bureau chief, was intrigued by a string of scoops I landed at *Roll Call*.

Alan and David rubbed each other the wrong way. So when

Alan heard David was pushing another candidate, I'm certain that put me over the top.

David redefined for me what it takes to be truly great:

☛ **UNCOMMON WORK ETHIC.** Every great athlete, writer, teacher, or leader works harder than others. There are no shortcuts or part-time paths to extreme betterment. David was notorious for being the person to open the reporters' gallery in the Capitol early each morning— and the last to leave. I made it my mission to be waiting there when he arrived and to leave after he left. He eventually wore me down. Work ethic is a powerful weapon.

☛ **DILIGENCE.** David's special gift is understanding the arcane congressional budgeting and appropriations process better than the lawmakers themselves and many of their staff members. Top leaders would routinely call him when arcane rules or historical precedents popped up. He spent decades reading, studying, asking questions. Digging deeply is a powerful weapon.

☛ **DOMAIN EXPERTISE.** Most lawmakers feared David and ducked his questions because they knew he could run circles around them. He wasn't cocky about it—just calm and certain that he saw and knew with total precision the full field. Domain expertise is a powerful weapon.

☞ **LOVE OF THE GAME.** David's hard exterior masks a poet's soul. His writing is lyrical. He labored over every sentence, summoning obscure historical figures or scenes and fighting editors down to the word, as if they were chipping at his being by trimming a preposition. But he poured so much reporting and thought into every sentence that every word did matter—to him. Caring profoundly is a powerful weapon.

☞ **HONOR.** David was a combat infantry medic in Vietnam, which shaped his character, beliefs, and journalism. It was the seminal experience of his life. David felt he owed it to those he served with to scrutinize the government and its operations. He also knew that people are policy. He spent an enormous amount of time trying to understand the people— lawmakers and staff—and what they were really like. Service and honor are powerful weapons.

THE BOTTOM LINE. You never saw David on TV or lighting up Twitter with hot takes. He was too busy doing the hard work in the trenches that it takes to be great—and setting a standard every reporter, every professional, should aspire to— even if we will never attain it.

PART 6

CHAPTER 61

HAPPINESS MATRIX

Sometimes when we're fighting, Autumn unleashes a teasing broadside about my theory for a sane life well lived: "Why don't you check your buckets on your stupid Happiness Matrix?" To rub it in, she throws air quotes around "Happiness Matrix."

WHY IT MATTERS. Roll your eyes all you want, folks. We all need a framework of *who* and *what* matters to us, and a mechanism for allocating sufficient times to each. Otherwise, life just throws us from meeting to meeting, obligation to obligation, and time-wasting distraction to time-wasting distraction.

We control more than most think—but only if we take ownership of that control. It took me until my forties to realize this fully. So hopefully you can do it sooner.

Think about it. Yes, you have a job and must-dos. But you alone control what you eat, whether you work out, who you call, who you spend time with, what hobbies bring you joy, what relationships enrich.

I track this with what I call my Happiness Matrix. I think of the buckets of life that bring me joy and meaning. I pay close attention to each bucket, and when things seem or feel off, it's often because one is empty or light.

Listing my buckets might help you create your own:

☞ **MY WIFE.** People are shocked that nearly half of marriages end in divorce. I am shocked *any* survive. It is hard to live with one person every day of every year. It takes constant work, humility, rhino-thick skin, and unconditional love and effort. With each passing year, I try to make this more of a priority. It pays off big-time. Except when I'm in the doghouse.

☞ **MY KIDS.** There is nothing I am prouder of than the unique, enjoyable, deep, and honest relationship I have with each of my three kids. I try to get the big things right with them—and to find one-on-one moments often, to talk about real stuff and to soak up their passions and problems. All three are my best friends now. But if I allow myself to get caught up in work or my personal obsessions, these relationships would suffer. And *I* would suffer.

☞ **MY PARENTS/SIBLINGS.** I won the lottery. My parents, siblings, and I love one another, enjoy one another, and suffer no weird family rivalries or bitterness. I talk to one or more of them near daily. But it's finding time to see them in person that dictates how full this bucket feels. This one always seems to have a hole in it.

☛ **MY FRIENDS.** I have a high threshold for close friends. Would they visit me if I had a stroke and were housebound? I try to put most of my free time into the half dozen who clear this bar, instead of hitting D.C. parties or looking for new friends. I try to finesse these relationships into deeper, meaningful ones. That's hard for most dudes, this one very much included. But it makes decisions about what to do with free time easier.

☛ **MY FAITH.** Life can feel empty when I'm thinking only of myself and my immediate needs. I think of my Christian faith as my gut check on whether I am living a life glorifying someone other than me or my family. It grounds me. It humbles me. It corrects me.

☛ **MY WORK.** This bucket is never dry. I am either working, thinking about work, or reacting to work, um, all the time. This is the one bucket I need to pound a hole in. But as you can tell, I love this shit.

☛ **MY HEALTH.** I make no apologies for carving out sixty to ninety minutes a day to work out. It baffles me that many do not. I am tireder, less sharp, and more agitated when I do not blow off steam with running, lifting, biking, or doing Pilates or yoga. And the older I get, the more disciplined I am about what I put into my body. Makes a massive difference.

☛ **MY HOBBIES.** My happy times are fly-fishing ocean flats for bonefish, hiking or four-wheeling the backwoods in Maine, clanking a 7 iron into the trees, being in the gym with my kids or with my wife on water, and doing anything outside, on the move. I am unapologetic about recharging with pure, selfish enjoyment.

CHAPTER 62

MEDITATE, MAN

All three Axios cofounders—Roy, Mike, and I—tried something we never imagined ourselves getting involved with: transcendental meditation (TM).

WHY IT MATTERS. We're perpetually in motion and distracted. If millions of people over thousands of years found peace and clearer minds with mantras and quiet meditation, why not us?

So we gave it a shot. All three of us took several classes in D.C. with Peter Lamoureux, a terrific TM teacher. The ceremonial stuff was weird but illuminating.

If nothing else, TM got us off life's Habitrail, if even for only a couple of twenty-minute chunks a day.

Put simply, TM is a meditative technique in which you silently repeat a mantra for twenty minutes while sitting with your eyes closed. You are given your own mantra—no, I will not tell you mine!

TM isn't a religion, a cult, a breathing exercise, or a celebrity fad. The stress-killing benefits of the practice can help all.

The David Lynch Foundation raises funds to provide meditation training to students, homeless people, veterans, and others for free. The scientific data behind TM is very persuasive.

The purpose of TM is to lift you out of your ordinary—often hectic—thinking process and into a state of restful alertness. The instructor gives you your own secret mantra—a simple sound or phrase to repeat. The repetition of it relaxes the mind and refreshes you, practitioners say.

For us, one of the most alluring parts of TM was the notion of unlocking brainpower that goes unused and improving our mental and physical health.

Our instructor described it as choppy waves atop a deep ocean—our brain being like an eighteen-foot boat being tossed on thirty-foot waves.

TM helps you "settle"—that's Mike's lightbulb word from the training—into deeper levels.

Lots of research shows the substantial benefits of TM, especially for people in high-stress jobs—frontline health workers or people who have suffered trauma, including veterans and survivors of sexual abuse.

Studies show TM can lessen anxiety, cut work stress, lower your risk of heart disease, and reduce your levels of cortisol, the stress hormone.

The instructor keeps telling us there's no right or wrong way to meditate (besides trying too hard). But let's face it—you get results or you don't.

The time commitment is real: TM practitioners insist on a four-session course taught by a trained professional. Then it's twenty minutes, twice a day.

THE BOTTOM LINE. Even if TM just gets us off our phones

for forty minutes a day, it's a massive success. But it's hard to stick with.

I kept at it for months but slowly fell out of practice. But to this day I will often carve out twenty minutes to try to jump-start the habit again.

Another practice worth trying is creative meditation, popularized by Stanford neuroscientist Andrew Huberman.

This type of meditation is designed to stimulate the creative and imaginative parts of the brain, which can lead to an increased flow of novel ideas.

The technique involves closing your eyes for five to ten minutes and visualizing a problem or situation that you want to solve or improve. You then try to generate as many different solutions or ideas as possible, without judging or censoring them.

The trick is to let your mind wander freely—and to be aware of, but not consumed with, feelings or thoughts.

Give both methods a spin for a few months. Write down the results. It might stick as a lifelong habit.

CHAPTER 63

EXTREME DISCIPLINE

Achieving insane success at work or in personal quests often requires extreme effort and discipline.

WHY IT MATTERS. Almost every person at the top of their game—be it sports or business—does extraordinary things to get their mind and body to perform optimally and at a higher level than others. People too often lose sight of how much of life—your health, your happiness, your smarts, your career—you steer. This can be a lazy and unwise mentality.

Yes, this is much easier for people with money, power, or free time. But I'm convinced it applies to all of us, because some of the most effective exercises are free—squats, planks, slow jogs, stretching.

Until my early twenties, I was about as unhealthy as you could be. I drank copious amounts of beer ... lived on burgers, corn dogs, and pizza ... smoked ... and rarely worked out.

I also started experiencing the early signs of ankylosing spondylitis, a rare disease that eventually leaves your entire spine fused and inflexible. The pain and immobility are often debilitating. I was stiff as the Tin Man, and my back often locked up so tightly I could not move.

My grandfather had the same disease. In the late 1960s, he slipped on ice, fracturing his back diagonally. He was told by several doctors he would never walk again. But one doctor was aware of AS and my grandfather's fully fused spine. The doctor surmised that since it was fused before the accident, my grandfather could lie facedown for six months and his spine would fuse back the same. The doctor was right. My grandfather was active into his eighties.

I was bummed but not surprised to learn I had AS, too. So I tracked down one of the world's leading experts on AS in search of a cure, only to find none exists. But I did discover a few studies showing Pilates—and exceptional inner core strength—can mitigate the pain and can offset the inflexibility.

I asked the doctor what would happen if I simply never sat still again, worked out constantly, mastered Pilates, and basically kept my spine in constant motion to complicate any fusing. He said go for it.

Now here I am, in my fifties. My lower and upper spine are fused, but I am active as hell (biking, hiking, running, lifting, Pilates, yoga, core) and rarely if ever in pain. This opened my eyes to the benefits of extreme discipline.

Most people doing extraordinary things weren't simply born with a gift—they learned grit and hard, meticulous work.

Here's how extreme discipline might apply to different parts of your life:

☛ **OUR DIETS.** There are countless good ones, but let's face it—most boil down to *reducing bad things* (sugar, simple carbs, booze, processed food) and *increasing good things* (more water, greens, fiber, healthy proteins—peas, eggs, fish). Try discipline for one week and measure how you feel.

☛ **OUR FAITH/MIND.** It's hard to center your brain and soul without some daily meditation, prayer, reflection. I try to meditate or pray to start or end my day. For me, this works only when I am extremely disciplined about it.

☛ **OUR BODIES.** Every person should find a *daily* exercise habit, even if it's walking, squats, planks, or biking. The body and mind vastly underperform without it. Start young to make it an extreme habit. But better to start now than tomorrow.

☛ **OUR CAREERS.** All the above give you a massive edge at work. But if you really want to crush the thing you spend the vast majority of your hours doing, you need to be more disciplined than others and demand more of yourself. There is no easy way to be great. But focus on *how y*ou work to sharpen your performance.

☛ **OUR GOODNESS.** This might seem an odd coda. But few things fuel contentment and inner joy more than giving to others. If you think about the benefits (helping others plus the psychic lift of doing so), it's a very efficient use of extreme discipline.

THE BOTTOM LINE. Start small—pick a passion to practice in this area for a few months. You'll find it gets increasingly easy to apply it to other parts of your life.

CHAPTER 64

WORK OUT

I was a lazy belly-builder into my twenties. Until I hit a literal bump.

I was driving from Oshkosh to Washington, D.C., hoping to catch my big break as a political journalist. Feeling carefree and confident, I was cruising along until I hit a big bump in the road.

Life suddenly slowed like a snail-motion scene in a movie... and my belly jiggled like a sack of jelly. Not sure why it surprised me: My lunch most days was three McDonald's cheeseburgers, supersize fries (I'm American, dammit), and an extra-large Mountain Dew. But it did.

WHY IT MATTERS. This one big shake of my beer belly inspired a thirty-year-plus journey to be in better physical shape every year than the previous one.

In small, halting steps, I achieved this. My first run, once I landed in D.C., was a heroic .25 mile around Jefferson Park. Yes, that's pathetic. But it was a start.

Since then, I have run half-marathons, conquered Pilates, lifted, biked, hiked, climbed, stretched, and tried every kind of class from Solidcore to boot camps.

I write this not to brag, but to show you that any one at any point can make the essential decision to take care of their body, regardless of ability.

● **TRUTH BOMB.** The consequences of not doing this are profound. You will feel worse physically and mentally, increase your chances of illness and pain, and fail to prep your body to fight off everything from colds to cancer. You also cement the likelihood that old age is less active and fun.

Some hacks that helped me:

☞ **START SMALL.** Can you run or swim one lap, lift light weights, or bike for twenty minutes *today*? Don't fixate on how hard it will be to lose twenty pounds or run a marathon. Stack small wins each day until you start to see bigger results first in mind, then later in body.

☞ **EXPERIMENT.** Find things you enjoy. Hike or jog scenic places. Or find a partner to lift weights with. Or join a yoga class with friends. You want it to be a treat, or at least tolerable, not a chore.

☞ **TAKE NOTES.** Change comes so slowly it can be imperceptible. You need reminders of the progress you are making. Also note how you feel, not just how you look.

☞ **MAKE IT A HABIT.** You need to shoot for thirty and ideally sixty minutes of exercise every day. Too many people aim the target too low. Don't. This means carving out time, prioritizing it, and getting off your butt when you want to slack. Give yourself grace when you skip it—but also give yourself a kick in the ass not to do it again.

☞ **NO EXCUSES.** Do *not* get into a one-exercise-only groove that you can't take on the road. Find things you can do *anywhere*. For instance, you can do push-ups, planks, squats, and jumping jacks in any place at any time. You need the chance to work out every day, regardless of where you are and what you're doing.

☞ **DIVERSIFY.** The meatheads at the gym pumping iron and squatting small buildings might be muscular. But I'm not sure they will fully benefit from the hard work. They are basically ballooning a few big muscles. Looks good. But your whole body needs attention. You get more long-term benefit by working different muscles in different ways. Lift. Walk. Bike. Hike. Stretch. Mix it up. Every study shows a mix of weights and cardio is best for you. Don't overthink the science.

☞ **MASTER *YOUR* BODY.** Pilates and/or yoga are essential to combat my spinal disease. Running, while invigorating, crushes my neck and right hip. Swimming elongates me. Climbing Mount Katahdin in Maine loosens my hips. I know all of this through trial and error and listening to my body. Do the same. What helps? What hurts? What genetic issues do you need to beat? Build your program around your specific needs.

☛ **SLOW DECLINE.** My annual goal is simply to be in better shape than I was the year before. This might mean lifting more or lowering my heart rate or increasing my flexibility or tightening my core. To me, this helps slow or ease the aging process. And it also makes me the measurement, not concepts imposed by others.

CHAPTER 65

EAT BETTER

I grew up in Wisconsin, where potatoes soaked with butter and sour cream and smothered with cheese and cornflakes are considered a healthy vegetable. Our vitamin-rich fresh fish are bathed luxuriously in flour and bread, dropped in boiling oil, and then dipped into thick lumps of mayo.

WHY IT MATTERS. Let's just say I wasn't born a health nut. Most of us aren't. We simply swallow stuff that tastes yummy. But it might be one of the dumbest things our species does en masse.

This is the part where you roll your eyes and say Jim is a judgmental jerk, hell-bent on shaming you. Screw him!

Well, the truth sometimes hurts and is very hard to hear. But I can't sugarcoat how hard it is to live, work, and play optimally if you don't stop pouring piles of crap into your gullet.

You don't have to be a preachy plant-eating vegan. You do have to understand food drives your health, energy, sleep, self-confidence, longevity, and mental sharpness. Sorry, this is not debatable.

Again, until my twenties, I bet my diet was way, way worse than yours.

This was my typical day: Get up early and hit McDonald's or Burger King for three breakfast sandwiches consisting of the holy trinity of eggs, cheese, and meat, smooshed between a buttery croissant.

If I was broke, the Captain stepped in. Cap'n Crunch, soaked in 2 percent milk, ripped apart my mouth and sent me on a sugary high. Lunch was those three McDonald's cheeseburgers, coupled with fries and a sugary soda the size of a bucket. Dinner was usually pizza, often a fourteen-inch Domino's loaded with God's greatest protein, pepperoni. At night, I pounded beers and devoured chips.

So I was basically jamming tubes of cholesterol into my arteries, superpowered by 5,000 calories of miscellaneous mystery meats and white-flour carbs, lubricated with lots of Rhinelander beer. No wonder my belly jiggled so merrily.

If I could kick this habit, surely you can, too. I am more militant today about food than necessary. But what I have learned in my journey might help:

- ☞ **START SIMPLE.** If you think about the enormity of losing a lot of weight or radically shifting your diet, you won't. Start small. Try to eat well *today.* And then for a full week . . . then longer. Maybe stop drinking sugary soda. Be aware of what you are putting into your body: Does this thing make it harder to feel or look better? Is there a healthier but not disgusting alternative?

- ☞ **RESIST SHORTCUTS.** Not eating for several days or gulping down diet pills is foolish. The way to shift habits and weight is slowly and consistently. Anything that sounds easy is BS. Fad diets are almost always a scam.

☞ **TAKE NOTES.** Write down how you feel physically and mentally as you change things. Progress is imperceptibly slow in the moment but substantial over time. You need a mechanism to record your progress.

☞ **FORGIVE. DON'T FORGET.** The road to better health is bumpy. Don't beat yourself up when you slip. Play the long game. Slow and steady. But also don't forget to bounce back fast.

☞ **NO LAST HURRAHS.** I was always guilty of this one. If I slipped for a long weekend (or much longer), I would tell myself, *One last binge of greasy pizza or bag of chips before I get back to eating healthy.* This is such a moronic mentality: It simply means you will need to work that much harder or longer to feel better.

☞ **GO NATURAL.** Processed foods are garbage—arguably the worst human invention for healthy living. Cut them out as much as possible. If it's not real, reject it.

☞ **LISTEN TO YOUR BODY.** You will soon learn your body screams what it really wants and needs. Sugar makes it sluggish. Carbs make it jones for more carbs. Booze makes its head hurt. The flip side: Lean proteins, veggies and healthy grains make it smile.

☛ **KEEP IT SIMPLE.** A healthy diet is easier than most think. There's a reason the Mediterranean diet is routinely found to be the healthiest. It's a simple mix of fish, lean proteins, healthy veggies, and grains. Don't overthink the obvious. My simple rule: Is this going to do a lot more good than bad for my body?

☛ **BUILD BACK BETTER.** You will soon find your mind, body, and soul operate more optimally. Build off the momentum. Find what foods actually make you feel better and more alive, and indulge in them. Mine are salmon, avocado, eggs, and artichokes. You're not going to plan a Super Bowl party around this menu. But it's tasty.

☛ **LOSE THE BOOZE.** This is a gut punch and struggle for me. I like drinking. Always have. Still do (though a lot less). But the idea that drinking can be healthy is BS—a myth spread by beverage companies and wishful thinkers. Any amount of booze is bad for your health. This doesn't mean you need to quit cold turkey. But it does mean you should start pulling back, the sooner the better.

CHAPTER 66

CHOOSE JOY

It often takes health scares or tragedy to focus your mind on the durable, indelible good stuff—including joy.

WHY IT MATTERS. Joy isn't simply a by-product of good times. It can be an active choice in crappy ones, a North Star.

My family lived this lesson in 2022. And it brought to the surface simple, surprising lessons applicable to all.

Autumn had endured a hellish medical journey all too familiar to too many. It started with one of those long-COVID horror stories you hear about—the brain fog, the piercing migraines, and the stroke-like episodes. It rendered a voracious reader unable to read and an eloquent speaker often unable to string words together.

Then her entire digestive system shut down, landing us in and out of a half dozen hospitals.

Emergency surgeries, months-long hospital stays, close calls, and ICU visits gave way to inexplicable drops in blood pressure, malnutrition, and frequent falls.

There were a few points where I feared this would not end well.

But something magical happened amid the chaos and unimaginable pain: Autumn seemed more at peace and was able to find hope and solace in overstuffed, understaffed rooms.

I was a hot mess. So at one point, I asked her how it was that she was not more demoralized.

"I choose joy," she said.

Autumn explained something that I've heard her say before in other contexts: While our life right now was suddenly very small and stressful, the one thing she could control was her joy.

She found it, she said, in me, in our kids who rose heroically to the moment, and in the friends and family who showed attentiveness, often in surprising ways.

She is right. Three things struck me that all of us can practice in tough times:

- ☛ **SAVOR WHAT YOU'VE GOT.** Autumn and I have been married twenty-two years. Neither of us is remotely easygoing: We are intense, opinionated, and sure of ourselves. We didn't marry our opposites. We married ourselves. I often joked I married me with boobs. But we've never found more joy in each other than in the solitary confinement of hospital rooms. We talked for hours, and I savored rubbing lotion on her dry legs without distraction.

- ☛ **DEEPEN WHAT YOU'VE GOT.** None of us wish pain on our kids. But we found new depths in our children. A good trick we learned over the years is not to hide the tough stuff, but instead to use it to deepen connections. We talk openly and honestly about the reality.

I watched my daughter spend hours reading to her mother, soothing her when she couldn't read.

I saw my sons prioritize after-school visits to the hospital, stretched out on their mom's bed trying to make her laugh. All three of them gathering strength before the surgeries to remind their mom that she's a warrior.

☞ **REDISCOVER WHAT YOU'VE GOT.** Nothing reveals the depth of friends more than how they rise to the awful moments. This is such a great tell for who really has your back. The most delightful discoveries are those who surprise you. And we were blessed with lots of surprises.

THE BOTTOM LINE. Try to choose joy, even when things suck or seem scary. The good stuff is often buried in the bad stuff.

As of the writing of this book, Autumn is very much on the rebound, exercising again, traveling, and making fun of my Happiness Matrix. Her long COVID persists, so she has rough periods, with piercing migraines and a cloudy mind. And her stomach may never be fully normal or settled. But she's alive—and still trying to choose joy.

CHAPTER 67

MIRACLE MAN

In 2018, a fourteen-year-old boy who had lost both parents dropped abruptly into our laps.

We knew Kelvin Martinez Membreno from years earlier, when he played soccer with our son, James. But we had mostly lost contact.

Yet here he was, asking if we would take him in. He had run away and was flirting with a dangerous lifestyle, and claimed living in his current situation was untenable. Four days later, he was at our door—a box with a birth certificate and other papers in hand, and a suitcase with all his clothes.

WHY IT MATTERS. Your life is defined not by preplanned ideas but by wild twists of unimaginable fate. How you handle these unexpected moments shapes your character and destiny.

A framework that helped me was thinking of our adopting Kelvin—like a start-up. You take a big risk few others try, brace for jarring ups and downs, lean on others—and recognize that failure is very possible, but not an option.

Kelvin was in a dark place when we met him—rarely at school, often in trouble. He struggled with behavioral issues, depression, and volatility.

When Kelvin was taking his first high school journalism class and agreed to share his story, he put it this way: "I was lost, insecure, sad, skipping school and making bad choices."

But his tender heart, probing mind, and genuine interest in others served as beacons on a path to hope.

During Kelvin's three experiences with inpatient treatment centers in three states, we often worried we were putting too much stress on our other two kids and our marriage.

No one changes fast, especially a kid who feels unloved and unwanted. You have to brace yourself for very difficult moments and have faith the small things will one day make a big difference.

"I had never talked about my parents dying. I had to pretend it never happened," Kelvin says. "It made me angry because I was keeping everything inside. So when it popped, it really popped."

Here are some basics that helped us:

- ☛ **GET THE FUNDAMENTALS RIGHT.** In starting and running two companies, I obsess about the foundational core being strong, then lean hard on it when tough times hit.

  Adoption was similar. You need to have a clear set of boundaries and expectations, teach and live them yourself, and bind yourself to them tightly in chaos.

- ☛ **LOVE IS YOUR SECRET SAUCE**. You need to say it and show it, relentlessly. You have to summon the truest form of unconditional love: Expect no reciprocation in the short term.

You need to imagine losing both parents or feeling totally abandoned. It makes love seem elusive, unattainable. The door to a happy, functional life opens only after one lets love in. And only then can one show it.

Often the anger, the self-medication, the running away are simply cries for love someone doesn't yet know how to experience. Cling to that.

☛ **BUILD A TEAM.** Autumn and I might have buckled if we hadn't put together a large network of friends and family: our other kids, who rose heroically to the moment; Kelvin's biological extended family, who stayed involved; a wonderful therapist; and generous friends.

Kelvin says his world started to turn for the better on his sixteenth birthday, when first his biological uncle, then members of our family, and then Kelvin himself offered tearful toasts to his slow but steady progress. "It was the first time I felt true love," Kelvin said. "I felt it was a resetting."

☛ **NEVER LOSE HOPE.** Kelvin is now nineteen. He is on the honor roll and a star on his high school soccer team, and behaves (mostly). He is committed to play soccer at the number one ranked (as of September 25,

2023) Division 3 soccer school in the country, Messiah University.

☛ **WHAT YOU PUT OUT COMES BACK.** Kelvin feels and shows love. He confidently talks about his journey, brims with gratitude, and lights up a room with his kindness and cheer. Today he proudly carries the name Kelvin Membreno VandeHei.

THE BOTTOM LINE. There will be many more twists and turns to this story. But this much is certain: Autumn, our other two kids, and I all count adding Kelvin to our Family Five as the best, most meaningful thing we ever did.

You often get more, grow more, feel more than the person you bring in. Even in the most painful moments, beautiful things are revealed.

CHAPTER 68

GIVE BIG

Nancy Economou is a kind, affable middle-aged single mother of five boys from the Chicago suburbs.

She's also likely delivered more free solar light to more poor women in more poor nations than any other person in America.

WHY IT MATTERS. Her life is a living lesson on how ordinary people can do extraordinary things with entrepreneurial ambition and thinking.

She cooked up her own not-for-profit start-up after discovering that in the poorest of poor villages, young women have little access to something all of us take for granted—light. That's not a typo.

If you live in the remote villages of the Philippines or in Malawi, where we visited, light is expensive (kerosene fuel or batteries aren't free), dangerous (kerosene easily spills or splatters and burns), and unavailable to many when the sun goes down.

So Economou created Watts of Love to bring safe, free, individual solar lights to tens of thousands of women, so they can work or learn at night.

She then teaches them the simplest of economics—the trickle-down effect of saving money to buy, say, a live chicken, which can lay eggs, which can feed their kids or be sold for money to buy a goat.

Each light is a small square, fully modified for the realities of living in a remote village.

One light costs roughly $20 to produce in China, at the cheapest supplier Economou can find. It costs $50 all in to deliver and pay locals to help teach.

One side is the light. On the other side is a sun-soaking solar panel for recharging.

On a full charge, the device runs 120 hours on reading-light bright, much less on fuller illumination modes.

A clever twist: It has a versatile strap, not a folding stand. So it can be affixed to your head or body during daytime to charge on the go, and to your head or hut for work at night.

Each one is designed to last a decade.

It's wild to visit people who received lights months ago and hear them tell their success stories.

I brought my two sons to witness Nancy's work and to help deliver and explain the lights. A lesson in leadership unfolded, too—full of tips for all of us.

- ☛ **TRUST YOUR GUT.** Nancy convinced herself a safe, user-friendly light improves lives, one at a time. She plunged in after her family lost almost everything in the housing crash. Given Nancy's situation, a single mom with five kids, *risky* was a wild understatement.

- ☛ **THINK BIG, START SMALL.** She started by traveling with a few boxes of bulkier lights and taught a few local women how to use them. She quickly found a fit between product and market: the women needed the lights and used them as envisioned. She started patenting her product.

☛ **SCALING MATTERS.** Economou soon realized that her setup—one American with a pallet of boxes in a foreign land—was terribly inefficient. She realized she needed smaller lights to maximize the number she could cram into boxes. More important, she needed a franchise model. So she adopted a "lighthouse strategy" to enlist and pay local leaders to help distribute and explain the lights. It's working.

☛ **SHINE.** As is true of any successful entrepreneur, her belief in her product is contagious. That has brought us and many others here. It has also attracted about $1.7 million in funding to spread the light. Like any ambitious entrepreneur, she's looking for donors to expand her enterprise to at least five times the size. The total addressable market (TAM, in start-up speak) is sadly almost unlimited.

THE BOTTOM LINE. The best part of the trip was watching how people light up when someone cares enough to simply show up—and show interest. A good life lesson is tucked in there.

CHAPTER 69

FAITH

I am not one to preach or talk much about my faith. Blame it on my Catholic reticence.

But there is one sentence, one verse, that captures my belief in what animates me as a leader and person. It's Corinthians 15:10:

> **But by the grace of God I am what I am, and his grace toward me has not been in vain. On the contrary, I worked harder than any of them, though it was not I but the grace of God that is with me.**

This was written by Paul after his famous Road to Damascus conversion from killer of Christians to the most prolific apostle and New Testament author.

WHY IT MATTERS. If you've read this far into the book, you see how miraculous it is that I've made it this far as a leader. I never forget that. And I never doubt there's a purpose to the work that I do. This gives me a self-confidence that transcends any gifts or brainpower, limitations or setbacks.

I consider myself an anti-denomination, struggling Christian. I grew up Catholic, went to Catholic schools K–12, and still admire parts of the church. But it's also an institution that has destroyed lives in unpardonable ways and too often puts its earthly power above its solemn responsibilities.

It's the same with the Anglican church I now attend sporadically. All institutions run by humans inevitably turn corrupt. So I think of church merely as a quiet place to pray and reflect, and don't expect much more of a building or a manmade institution.

You don't need to be a person of faith to be a great person. But you do need to find deep meaning in your work and life. You also need the humility to realize whatever gifts you have were passed on to you by someone (parents, coaches, friends, mentors) or something (God, karma, genetics).

Here's a framework for finding your grounding in something beyond:

☛ **FIND A FAITH.** I just don't see how you finish life's race victorious if there is not a higher being or a deeper meaning. This can be as grand as an all-powerful God or as mystical as karma. But take the time to reflect on spirituality or secular connectedness. In the end, it's not about you.

☛ **PRACTICE IT.** Carve out time for reflection, prayer, or meditation. Start small if you are skeptical. The Mister Rogers exercise of taking a few minutes to quietly name—and be grateful for—all the people who have helped or touched you over the year is a wonderful start. Then slowly explore why they fell into your life, what motivated them, what unites us, and how you can make it onto someone else's gratitude list.

☛ **BE TOLERANT.** Being a believer in anything is hard enough. Being judged for it only makes it harder. I am a Christian, but I am also a freethinking skeptic smart enough to realize I might be wrong. Some Christians will balk at that sentence. But it's true. All we can do is follow our hearts and minds and give others the space to do the same.

☛ **LOVE, MAN.** This is universal. Almost every faith is centered on a love bigger than ourselves. We can show this daily with humility by serving others, forgiving others, performing acts of charity, and spreading joy. Spoiler alert: This *always* makes you feel better. It's why we're here.

☛ **TRY NEW THINGS.** I have taken meditation, yoga, fasting, and the Mister Rogers exercise routine—daily laps in the pool—out for spins and found all four beneficial. Rigid thinking creates dull minds . . . and lives.

CHAPTER 70

THE GOOD STUFF

My life is littered with mistakes:

- I wasted most of high school and college in a partying haze.

- I was arrested twice and jailed once for disorderly conduct.

- I spent half my life drinking and eating crap.

- I have blown countless hours at war with rivals and a few former friends.

- I too often lost my shit when my kids did something bone-headed.

But I learned something from every dumb move and used it to try to get the Big Things right.

WHY IT MATTERS. Five decades in, that is what matters most to me: getting the big things right. That seems like a worthy goal for all of us: cut ourselves slack on our daily sins or stumbles and make sure we nail the Big Stuff. The Big Stuff is the Good Stuff.

My Good Stuff list is fairly simple:

1. Deep meaningful, unconditional relationships with my kids.

2. A healthy, resilient marriage.

3. Strong, loving relationships with my parents and siblings.

4. A few deep and durable friendships.

5. Faith and connection beyond myself.

6. Doing consequential work with people I enjoy and admire.

So, how do you nail the big and good stuff?

☞ **IDENTIFY IT.** This is an evolving list, often shaped by time and circumstance. But we should all have our Good Stuff list in our head or on paper. It keeps ya focused. It grounds you when chaos and crisis hits. And it will hit, often.

☞ **TRY.** Marriage is hard, sometimes impossibly so. Parents and siblings and friends can be terrific pains in the ass. Work is often a grind and full of disappointment. So you need to work your tail off, especially in tough times, to learn, then forget and then make big things better, slowly and durably. In Pink's immortal words: "Try, try, try."

☛ **HAVE SOME GRACE.** Grace for others. Grace for yourself. We're all deeply flawed, wounded, selfish, clueless, and mean at different times. It does not make us bad. It makes us normal. Forgiveness is a powerful cure.

☛ **PLAY THE LONG GAME.** Bad news: I can promise you your big things will feel like big failures many—and sometime most—days. The good stuff will feel like bad stuff. I have blown many months beating myself up for being a selfish husband or an inattentive son or a harsh leader or an absent friend. And all those things were often true! But life is not measured by a moment.

☛ **FINISH STRONG.** We will all die. That will be our judgment day, in both a religious and a secular sense. We will sit there in those final hours and reflect. A worthy coda would be to say with supreme and sublime confidence: I learned a little every day, tried to do the next right thing, and got the Big Things right.

That, my friends, is the very definition of the Good Stuff.

ACKNOWLEDGMENTS

Well, let's do a blast of bullets to thank the people who made this possible:

- My parents, John and Joan, and siblings, Johnny and Julie, for a life of unconditional love and fun. Thank you for making me normal-ish.

- My wife, Autumn, for loving, guiding, and tolerating me—and making me a better dude. Oh, and inspiring much of this book.

- My kids, Sophie, James, and Kelvin, for letting me exploit them for stories and life lessons. And for being my best friends.

- Mike Allen, for inspiring and shaping much of this book—and making work and life a blast.

- Roy Schwartz, for being not just a best friend but also the frickin' business genius who helped me get paid a lot doing something I would do for free.

- Every Axios colleague, past and present. Your smarts and passion keep the juices flowing.

- To Axios readers and anyone bored enough to read acknowledgments: thank you for reading and caring.

- To every person mentioned in this book for filling my life with wild and wonderful stories.

- Rafe Sagalyn, my agent. This dude rocks. He dreamt up the idea of our first book and pushed me to do this one, too. If you're thinking of writing a book, hire him.

- Shannon Welch, my editor. Let's face it: I am an odd duck with a different writing style. She embraced and encouraged it—and then made me better and fit for public consumption. If you're writing a book, beg her to edit it.

- Matthew Benjamin, my closing editor, who stepped in late in the game to land this plane without crashing.

- All those people pissed I forgot to mention them: Focus on the Good Stuff!

SMART BREVITY ON JIM VANDEHEI

1971 Born in Oshkosh, Wisconsin, where a guidance counselor at his Catholic high school told him he had zero chance of getting into college.

1996– Worked his way up in traditional media in Washington—
2006 from the trenches of *New Fuels Report* and *Roll Call* to the glory of the *Wall Street Journal* and the *Washington Post.*

2007 Cofounded *Politico*, the game-changing political site.

2016 Named national editor of the year, then quit *Politico.*

2017 Cofounded and become CEO of Axios, a revolutionary news organization aimed at making people smarter, faster on the topics that matter most.

2022 Sold Axios for $525 million, to Cox Enterprises of Atlanta.

2022 Coauthor of *Smart Brevity: The Power of Saying More with Less,* a *Wall Street Journal* bestseller that unpacks the Axios secret sauce to help every reader communicate more powerfully.